THE
GOSPEL OF
JOHN:
DISPENSATIONALLY CONSIDERED

A GRACE EXPOSITIONAL COMMENTARY

Dr. David Alan Greene

GraceWord Publishing, LLC
www.gracewordpublishing.com
U.S.A.

Contents

To B'nai Avraham — the children of Abraham

Now I say that
Jesus Christ
was a minister of the circumcision
for the truth of God,
to confirm the promises
made unto the fathers:

– The Apostle Paul

Acknowledgements

I would like to express a special thanks to Jon and Susan McMahon and Frances Greene for their continued encouragement. To those who assisted with the preparation of this book, I offer my gratitude.

Introduction

This introduction will play a key role in understanding the Gospel of John. The reader should be familiar with the concept and application of rightly dividing the Word of Truth. It is also known as the dispensational approach to Scripture. To summarize, when God ordered the Bible, He divided it into ages or dispensations. Each of these divisions were intended to lead towards God's ultimate goal of restoring His Creation.

Traditionally, the Bible has been divided into seven ages or periods of time. Sometimes, these divisions are referred to as administrations in which God chose to make Himself known. There is a progression in these administrations which leads to its conclusion. Jumping into the middle of a book or movie series does not allow the reader to fully enjoy or understand the series in full.

GraceWord Publishing created the Grace Expositional Bible Commentary. Each commentary walks the reader through the Bible verse-by-verse. This is done while applying a system or method of interpretation. For this reason, I recommend the reader be familiar with the simple concept of "rightly dividing the Word of Truth" as Paul instructed Timothy. 2 Timothy 2:15:

> 15 **Study to shew thyself approved unto God, a workman that needeth not to be ashamed, <u>rightly dividing the word of truth.</u>**

To understand any portion of Scripture, it must be seen in its proper perspective. It is dangerous to take verses of Scripture out of its context. By doing so, there is a high risk of missing the point and not knowing to whom the message was intended.

Like the number of days that God took to create the earth, the Bible can be seen in seven periods of time or ages or dispensations in which He redeems His Creation. Looking at the four gospels as a group, they open in the middle of the fifth dispensation which is the Age of Law. The Jews received the Law from Moses. God used him to lead His people out of Egypt. It was during their sojourn in the Wilderness that God created a peculiar or special people or a holy nation separated from the other nations. These people had a specific purpose. God told Moses to speak to the people. Exodus 19:6:

> 6 **And ye shall be unto me <u>a kingdom of priests, and an holy nation</u>. These are the words which thou shalt speak unto the children of Israel.**

God had an ultimate purpose for these people and they will play a key role in His restored Creation.

Through Moses, God offered the children of Abraham, Isaac, and Jacob a binding contract or covenant. God would contractually obligate His people. In the verses that follow, notice His offer and their acceptance. The people bound themselves to this conditional agreement. Verses 7-8:

> 7 **And Moses came and called for the elders of the people, and laid before their faces all these words which the LORD commanded him.**

> 8 <u>**And all the people answered together, and said, All that the LORD hath spoken we will do.**</u> **And Moses returned the words of the people unto the LORD.**

This agreement or covenant still remains in effect today. This fact is important because nothing has changed for the Jews since the day they voluntarily accepted the terms of this agreement.

This means that the Law was in full effect throughout Jesus' earthly ministry. Consider His words in the Sermon of the Mount where the multitude of Jews gathered to hear Him speak. Matthew 5:17-18:

> 17 **Think not that I am come to destroy the law, or the prophets: I am not come to destroy, but to fulfil.**
>
> 18 **For verily I say unto you, Till heaven and earth pass, one jot or one tittle shall in no wise [way] pass from the law, till [it] all be fulfilled.**

So, the Law will be fulfilled at the end of the restoration. It will be Jesus Christ Who fulfills the Law for them.

Even after His death and resurrection, those who follow the Gospel of the Kingdom remain bound to the Law. Consider the words of the Apostle James who wrote to the children of Abraham as they await the return of their Messiah. Look how John addresses them. In his letter, he seeks to comfort and encourage the Kingdom Believers. James 1:1:

1 James, a servant of God and of the Lord Jesus Christ, <u>to the twelve tribes which are scattered abroad, greeting.</u>

Knowing to whom James wrote this letter reveals something important. It makes clear that the Law is still in effect for the Jews who follow the Gospel of the Kingdom. James, who was one of the Twelve, wrote in verse 2:10:

10 For whosoever shall keep the whole law, and yet offend in one point, he is guilty of all.

James does not inform them but remind them of their obligation according to the Mosaic Covenant. The entire Law was read aloud to those in the Wilderness. Consider, again, their response. Exodus 19:8:

8 And <u>all the people answered together, and said, All that the LORD hath spoken we will do</u>. And Moses returned the words of the people unto the LORD.

The first five books of the Bible are called the "books of Moses." In the fifth book, Deuteronomy, there was a portion of the Mosaic Covenant which is referred to as the "blessings and curses." It is clear from this that the covenant is conditional. If they obey and do what is right according to the covenant, God will bless them. However, if they break just one point of the covenant, God will curse or punish them. James reiterates this point in his letter to them. He reminds them of their commitment to this covenant.

We will look at two portions of Scripture. The first refers to the blessings. Deuteronomy 28:1-2:

> 1 **And it shall come to pass, if thou shalt hearken diligently unto the voice of the LORD thy God, to observe and to do all his commandments which I command thee this day, that the LORD thy God will set thee on high above all nations of the earth:**
>
> 2 **And <u>all these blessings shall come on thee, and overtake thee, if thou shalt hearken unto the voice of the LORD thy God</u>.**

The second are the consequences for failing to keep the Law in its entirety. Verse 15:

> 15 **But it shall come to pass, <u>if thou wilt not hearken unto the voice of the LORD thy God, to observe to do all his com-</u>**

mandments and his statutes which I command thee this day; that all these curses shall come upon thee, and overtake thee:

Notice in both references, the word "all" plays a key part in the effect it has upon the children of Abraham, Isaac, and Israel.

From Moses, King David, King Solomon, and all the Old Testament prophets, the Law of Moses remains in effect. Nothing changed when Jesus was born. The Apostle Paul tells us that Jesus was under the Law and His purpose was to redeem those who were under the Law. Galatians 4:4-5:

4 But when the fulness of the time was come, God sent forth his Son, made of a woman, made under the law, 5 To redeem them that were under the law, that we might receive the adoption of sons.

There is more to the Old Testament that will have a lasting effect on the people. In addition to the Mosaic Covenant, there are other covenants made with both Abraham and King David that continue. The Jews were taught and knew these promises. It gave them hope for their future because they trusted that God would fulfill them. Both of the following covenants are unconditional. This means that the responsibility is on God to fulfill these promises. Here, they are summarized.

Abrahamic Covenant:

This is found in Genesis 12:1-3:

1 **Now the LORD had said unto Abram, Get thee out of thy country, and from thy kindred, and from thy father's house, unto a land that I will shew thee:**

2 **And <u>I will make of thee a great nation, and I will bless thee, and make thy name great; and thou shalt be a blessing</u>:**

3 **And <u>I will bless them that bless thee, and curse him that curseth thee</u>: and in thee shall all families of the earth be blessed.**

Davidic Covenant:

God had the prophet Nathan deliver this message to King David. 2 Samuel 7:12-13:

12 **And when thy days be fulfilled, and thou shalt sleep with thy fathers, <u>I will set up thy seed after thee</u>, which shall proceed out of thy bowels, <u>and I will establish his kingdom.</u>**

13 **He shall build an house for my name, and <u>I will stablish the throne of his kingdom for ever.</u>**

We see in the following that the Seed or "Son of David" will be Jesus Christ. Verses 14-16:

14 **<u>I will be his father, and he shall be my son.</u> If he commit iniquity, I will chasten him with the rod of men, and with the stripes of the children of men:** 15 **<u>But my mercy shall not depart away from him</u>, as I took it from Saul, whom I put away before thee.**

16 **<u>And [through Him] thine house and thy kingdom shall be established for ever before thee: thy throne shall be established for ever.</u>**

Having an understanding of these facts will add a deeper understanding of the Word of Truth. For the more advanced student, you may wish to consider reading *Letters To Theophilus: Are You Ready For The End Times?* Consider also *The Glorious Destiny of Israel: The Fulfillment of God's Promises and Prophecies to Israel.* These two books present two sides of the same coin from the perspective of both the non-Jew and Jew respectively. Others may enjoy reading an overall summary of the Bible found in *The Hidden Gospel.* It highlights key events in the Bible and explains how it all comes together in the end. As of this writing, some are available as audiobooks.

It is my hope that people will learn, understand, and enjoy their Bible.

1

About the Apostle John

The Apostle John wrote five books in the New Testament. These include the Gospel of John, three short epistles (1 John, 2 John, and 3 John) and the final book of the New Testament called Revelation. John was one of the Twelve and he was an eyewitness to what Jesus said and did during His ministry. John is considered to be part of the "inner circle" along with Peter and James. These three were witnesses of the Transfiguration. (See Matthew 17:1-9). John continued to carry on overseeing the ministry from Jerusalem. Many years later, in the meeting of the Twelve with the Apostle Paul, Paul described John as a pillar or leader in his Jerusalem meeting. Galatians 2:9:

> 9 **And when James, Cephas [Peter], and John, who seemed to be pillars, perceived the grace that was given unto me,**

they gave to me and Barnabas the right hands of fellowship; that we should go unto the heathen, and they unto the circumcision.

John and his brother James were the sons of Zebedee and Salome. They made their living as fisherman on the Sea of Galilee where Jesus found them mending nets. He called them and they followed Him throughout His earthly ministry. In the Gospel of Mark, the Twelve are listed by name. Notice Mark's reference to John and his brother James. Mark 3:17:

17 **And James the son of Zebedee, and John the brother of James; and he surnamed them Boanerges, which is, The sons of thunder:**

They were called the "Sons of Thunder" because of their brazen and often outspoken nature. They must have gotten that from their mother who approached Jesus on their behalf. There is a Yiddish word "hutzpah" which means "nerve, unbelievable gall or audacity." We see it in the question she asked Jesus. Matthew 20:20-23:

20 **Then came to him the mother of Zebedee's children with her sons, worshipping him, and desiring a certain thing**

of [from] him. 21 And he said unto her, What wilt thou? She saith unto him, Grant that these my two sons may sit, the one on thy right hand, and the other on the left, in thy kingdom.

22 But Jesus answered and said, Ye know not what ye ask. Are ye able to drink of the cup that I shall drink of, and to be baptized with the baptism that I am baptized with? They say unto him, We are able.

23 And he saith unto them, Ye shall drink indeed of my cup, and be baptized with the baptism that I am baptized with: but to sit on my right hand, and on my left, is not mine to give, but it shall be given to them for whom it is prepared of [by] my Father.

Jesus met James and John on the shore of Galilee where he called two other brothers, Simon Peter and Andrew. Matthew 4:18-22:

18 And Jesus, walking by the sea of Galilee, saw two brethren, Simon called Peter, and Andrew his brother, casting a net into the sea: for they were fishers.

19 And he saith unto them, Follow me, and I will make you fishers of men. 20 And they straightway left their nets, and followed him.

21 And going on from thence, he saw other two brethren, James the son of Zebedee, and John his brother, in a ship with Zebedee their father, mending their nets; and he called them. 22 And they immediately left the ship and their father, and followed him.

The Gospel of John ends with a particular reference to himself. Jesus had told Peter about his future. Referring to John, Peter basically asks Jesus, "But, what about him?" John 21:20-24:

20 Then Peter, turning about, seeth the disciple whom Jesus loved following; which also leaned on his breast at supper, and said, Lord, which is he that betrayeth thee? 21 Peter seeing him saith to Jesus, Lord, and what shall this man do?

22 Jesus saith unto him, If I will that he tarry till I come, what is that to thee? follow thou me. 23 Then went this saying abroad among the brethren, that that

disciple should not die: yet Jesus said not unto him, He shall not die; but, If I will that he tarry till I come, what is that to thee? 24 This is the disciple which testifieth of these things, and wrote these things: and we know that his testimony is true.

John was the youngest of the disciples and, as a result, he outlived the other apostles. It is believed that he died from natural causes around 100 AD. We find that, in later life, John spent his final years on the Isle of Patmos. This is a Greek island in the Aegean Sea off the west coast of Turkey. The following information comes from the book of Revelation where the book was written. Revelation 1:9:

9 I John, who also am your brother, and companion in tribulation, and in the kingdom and patience of Jesus Christ, was in the isle that is called Patmos, for the word of God, and for the testimony of Jesus Christ.

2

John 1

When we compare the Gospel of John with the other gospels, we notice a difference in its style. Matthew, Mark, and Luke are known as the synoptic gospels and present an historical narrative. The Gospel of John has a different purpose. John states his purpose of writing his gospel in John 20:31:

> **31 But these are written, that ye might believe that Jesus is the Christ, the Son of God; and that believing ye might have life through his name.**

This is the gospel that is recommended to new believers most often because it establishes Jesus' identity. Jesus is the Messiah, the Anointed One, and the Son of God.

With that, we are ready to begin. John 1:1-3:

1 In the beginning was the Word, and the Word was with God, and the Word was God.

2 The same was in the beginning with God. 3 All things were made by him; and without him was not any thing made that was made.

John begins by establishing that Jesus is the Almighty God, Creator of the Universe. This often becomes a problem with Jewish believers who have been taught the Shema since they were small. Deuteronomy 6:4-5:

4 Hear, O Israel: The LORD our God is one LORD: 5 And thou shalt love the LORD thy God with all thine heart, and with all thy soul, and with all thy might.

However, John's statement is true. John is writing to the children of Israel to whom the promises were made. Therefore, it is important for us to stop and consider the importance of John's statement.

In my discussions with traditional Jews, their problem with the Gospel of the Kingdom is they believe in only one God: the Creator of the Universe. How, then, can Jesus also be God? I like to give the response I gave my personal doctor who was a devout Jew. I asked if he was his father's son. Then, I asked if he was his wife's husband. Finally, I asked if he was the father of his children. To all of these questions, he answered "yes." Looking directly at him, I ask him if there were three of him or only one. It is the same with God: there are not three, but One. Another example I give has to do with the various states of water: ice, water, and steam. They are all water but in a different state. I am using simple examples to explain God. The testimony of John and the other writers of the gospels will support the deity of Jesus throughout His ministry.

Jesus and God share the same attributes for in both of them is life. John 1:4-5:

> 4 **In him was life; and the life was the light of men.** 5 **And the light shineth in darkness; and the darkness comprehended it not.**

The Prophet Isaiah foretold of the Messiah's Coming. Isaiah 7:14:

> 14 **Therefore the Lord himself shall give you a sign; Behold, a virgin shall conceive, and bear a son, and shall call his name Immanuel.**

The name Immanuel means "God with us." God sent a prophet ahead of His Son to herald His arrival, John the Baptist. His purpose was to announce His arrival. John 1:6-9:

> 6 There was a man sent from God, whose name was John. 7 The same came for a witness, to bear witness of the Light, that all men through him might believe.

> 8 He [John] was not that Light, but was sent to bear witness of that Light. 9 That was the true Light, which lighteth every man that cometh into the world.

The One Who created the universe and created the light had come to His own people. He was Immanuel. For Jesus was both the Son of Abraham and the Son of David. Yet, the religious leaders of Israel would reject Him. Verses 10-11:

> 10 He was in the world, and the world was made by him, and the world knew him not. 11 He came unto his own, and his own received him not.

Rejected by the religious leaders, He was accepted by the people. Those who were once dead in sin, the lost sheep of the house of Israel, could be redeemed. They were not born again of flesh and blood, but by the power and Spirit of God. Verses 12-13:

> 12 **But as many as received him, to them gave he power to become the sons of God, even [that is to say] to them that believe on his name:**

> 13 **Which were born, not of blood, nor of the will of the flesh, nor of the will of man, but of God.**

John makes an important point that all believers, both Kingdom Believers and Grace Believers, should remember. He makes a connection between Jesus, the Son of God, and Scripture which is the written Word of God. We can measure our love for Jesus by our love for the written Word of God. Remember this: Jesus is the incarnate Word of God! Verse 14:

> 14 **And the Word was made flesh, and dwelt among us, (and we beheld his glory, the glory as of the only begotten of the Father,) full of grace and truth.**

John the Baptist was sent in advance to be a witness for Jesus Christ. Verses 15-18:

11

15 John bare witness of him, and cried, saying, This was he of whom I spake, He that cometh after me is preferred before me: for he was before me.

16 And of his fulness have all we received, and grace for grace.

17 For the law was given by Moses, but grace and truth came by Jesus Christ.

18 No man hath seen God at any time; the only begotten Son, which is in the bosom of the Father, he hath declared him.

The words "the only begotten Son" refers to the unique nature of Jesus' resurrection. His resurrection makes Him the first to be born again from the dead. He is also first in preeminence. John remarks in the opening of Revelation. Verse 1:5:

5 And from Jesus Christ, who is the faithful witness, and <u>the first begotten of the dead</u> . . .

The Apostle John tells us how John the Baptist's ministry began. John 1:19-23:

19 And this is the record of John, when the Jews sent priests and Levites from Jerusalem to ask him, Who art thou? 20 And he confessed, and denied not; but confessed, I am not the Christ.

21 And they asked him, What then? Art thou Elias? And he saith, I am not. Art thou that prophet? And he answered, No.

22 Then said they unto him, Who art thou? that we may give an answer to them that sent us. What sayest thou of thyself?

23 He said, <u>I am the voice of one crying in the wilderness, Make straight the way of the Lord, as said the prophet Esaias.</u>

John the Baptist is the one who will fulfill the prophecy in Isaiah 40:3.

We were previously told that the religious leaders would reject the Messiah. This becomes evident from the very beginning. Verses 24-28:

24 And they which were sent were of

[from] the Pharisees. 25 And they asked him, and said unto him, Why baptizest thou then, if thou be not that Christ, nor Elias, neither that prophet?

26 John answered them, saying, I baptize with water: but there standeth one among you, whom ye know not; 27 He it is, who coming after me is preferred before me, whose shoe's latchet I am not worthy to unloose.

28 These things were done in Bethabara beyond Jordan, where John was baptizing.

John proclaims Jesus' arrival. Verses 29-30:

29 The next day John seeth Jesus coming unto him, and saith, <u>Behold the Lamb of God, which taketh away the sin of the world.</u>

30 This is he of whom I said, After me cometh a man which is preferred before me: for he was before me.

Jesus must take preeminence because, as Creator, He existed before John. Verses 31-32:

31 And I knew him not: but that he should be made manifest [made known] to Israel, therefore am I come baptizing with water.

32 And John bare record, saying, I saw the Spirit descending from heaven like a dove, and it abode upon him.

John the Baptist would baptize the Anointed One with water and receive a sign. Verses 33-34:

33 And I knew him not: but he that sent me to baptize with water, the same said unto me, Upon whom thou shalt see the Spirit descending, and remaining on him, the same is he which baptizeth with the Holy Ghost.

34 And <u>I saw, and bare record that this is the Son of God.</u>

John was told for Whom he should look. Yet, the Spirit testified to him Who the Anointed One was when he beheld Him. Verses 35-36:

35 Again the next day after John stood, and two of his disciples; **36** And looking upon Jesus as he walked, he saith, Behold the Lamb of God!

John the Baptist had his own disciples whom he taught. Two of them saw Jesus and followed Him. Verses 37-42:

37 **And the two disciples heard him speak, and they followed Jesus.**

38 **Then Jesus turned, and saw them following, and saith unto them, What seek ye? They said unto him, Rabbi, (which is to say, being interpreted, Master,) where dwellest thou?**

39 **He saith unto them, Come and see. They came and saw where he dwelt, and abode with him that day: for it was about the tenth hour.**

40 **One of the two which heard John speak, and followed him, was Andrew, Simon Peter's brother. 41 He first findeth his own brother Simon, and saith unto him, We have found the Messias, which is, being interpreted, the Christ [Messiah].**

42 **And he brought him to Jesus. And**

when Jesus beheld him, he said, Thou art Simon the son of Jona: thou shalt be called Cephas, which is by interpretation, a stone.

Jesus was baptized in the Jordan River in the area of Bethany. The Apostle John does not include the forty days that Jesus was tested in the wilderness. When He returned from that testing, He departed for the area of Galilee which includes the sea by the same name. This area was located in northern Israel. Verses 43-51:

43 The day following Jesus would go forth into Galilee, and findeth Philip, and saith unto him, Follow me.

44 Now Philip was of [from] Bethsaida, the city of Andrew and Peter. 45 Philip findeth Nathanael, and saith unto him, <u>We have found him, of whom Moses in the law, and the prophets, did write, Jesus of Nazareth, the son of Joseph.</u>

46 And Nathanael said unto him, Can there any good thing come out of Nazareth? Philip saith unto him, Come and see.

47 Jesus saw Nathanael coming to him, and saith of him, Behold an Israelite indeed, in whom [there] is no guile!

48 Nathanael saith unto him, Whence [Wherefrom] knowest thou me? Jesus answered and said unto him, Before that Philip called thee, when thou wast under the fig tree, I saw thee.

49 Nathanael answered and saith unto him, Rabbi, <u>thou art the Son of God;</u> <u>thou art the King of Israel.</u>

50 Jesus answered and said unto him, Because I said unto thee, I saw thee under the fig tree, believest thou? thou shalt see greater things than these.

51 And he saith unto him, Verily, verily, I say unto you, Hereafter ye shall see heaven open, and the angels of God ascending and descending upon the Son of man.

3

John 2

The following story is often shared at weddings. It is the first time Jesus performs a miracle much to the amazement of His mother and disciples. John 2:1-6:

1 And the third day there was a marriage in Cana of Galilee; and the mother of Jesus was there: 2 And both Jesus was called [invited], and his disciples, to the marriage.

3 And when they wanted wine, the mother of Jesus saith unto him, They have no wine. 4 Jesus saith unto her, Woman, what have I to do with thee? mine hour is not yet come. 5 His mother saith unto the servants, Whatsoever he saith unto you, do it.

6 And there were set there six waterpots of stone, after the manner of the purifying of the Jews, containing two or three firkins apiece.

For those in food service or catering, they call this the "back of the house" as it is hidden from the arriving guests. To set the scene, a firkin is a measurement of about eight gallons. Therefore, each of these six stone waterpots held between sixteen and twenty-four gallons each.

This was an important marriage. Jesus, his mother, family, friends, and the disciples were there. A shortage of wine would be a great embarrassment to the hosts of the party. Jesus was called upon by His mother, most likely providentially. Verses 7-11:

7 Jesus saith unto them, Fill the waterpots with water. And they filled them up to the brim.

8 And he saith unto them, Draw out now, and bear unto the governor of the feast. And they bare it.

9 When the ruler [master] of the feast had tasted the water that was made wine, and knew not whence it was: (but

the servants which drew the water knew;) the governor of the feast called the bridegroom,

10 And saith unto him, Every man at the beginning doth set forth good wine; and when men have well drunk, then that which is worse: but thou hast kept the good wine until now.

11 <u>This beginning of miracles did Jesus in Cana of Galilee, and manifested forth his glory; and his disciples believed on him.</u>

Since the time of the Law, Prophets, and Writings, the Jews expected God to validate His prophets by miracles, signs, and wonders. Since Israel lives in a pagan world, God authenticates His messengers. Verse 12:

12 After this he went down to Capernaum, he, and his mother, and his brethren, and his disciples: and they continued there not many days.

Since it was near to Passover, Jesus and His disciples went to Jerusalem. The other gospels do not include this event of His early life. Verses 13-17:

13 And the Jews' passover was at hand, and Jesus went up to Jerusalem, 14 And found in the temple those that sold oxen and sheep and doves, and the changers of money sitting:

15 And when he had made a scourge of small cords, he drove them all out of the temple, and the sheep, and the oxen; and poured out the changers' money, and overthrew the tables;

16 And said unto them that sold doves, Take these things hence; make not my Father's house an house of merchandise.

17 And his disciples remembered that it was written, The zeal of thine house hath eaten me up.

Later, at the end of His ministry, Jesus would come again to the Temple in a similar manner.

While at the Temple, Jesus began to teach the lost sheep of the house of Israel. Verses 18-20:

18 Then answered the Jews and said unto him, What sign shewest thou unto

us, seeing that thou doest these things?

19 Jesus answered and said unto them, Destroy this temple, and in three days I will raise it up.

20 Then said the Jews, Forty and six years was this temple in building, and wilt thou rear [raise] it up in three days?

Much of what He **taught concerning** His death and resurrection was not understood. Verses 21-22:

21 But he spake of the temple of his body. 22 When therefore he was risen from the dead, his disciples remembered that he had said this unto them; and they believed the scripture, and the word which Jesus had said.

However, this would change after He appeared to them in His risen body.

We sometimes forget that Jesus is Emmanuel — God with us. Jesus understood human nature. Many believed because of the miracles. However, their belief would soon fade and Jesus knew this. Some of those who believed would be like the morning dew upon the grass? By afternoon, it is all but gone.

Verses 23-25:

23 Now when he was in Jerusalem at the passover, in the feast day, many believed in his name, when they saw the miracles which he did.

24 But Jesus did not commit himself unto them, because he knew all men,

25 And needed not that any should testify of man: for he knew what was in man.

4

John 3 (Part I)

How we understand the Bible has a lot to do with understanding its words. The Bible was written with words that convey a meaning. What God reveals should be important to the reader. We must be sure not to miss it. Here is a grammatical fact we should know. In this chapter, you will see the importance of this. There is a rule for pronouns. They cannot stand alone and must refer back to a noun whether it be a person, place, or thing. When we see a pronoun used in Scripture, we must know to whom or what it refers. John 3:1-5:

> 1 **There was a man of the Pharisees, named Nicodemus, a ruler of the Jews:**
>
> 2 **The same came to Jesus by night, and said unto him, Rabbi, we know that thou art a teacher come from God: for no**

man can do these miracles that thou doest, except God be with him.

3 Jesus answered and said unto him, Verily, verily, I say unto thee, Except a man be born again, he cannot see the kingdom of God.

4 Nicodemus saith unto him, How can a man be born when he is old? can he enter the second time into his mother's womb, and be born?

5 Jesus answered, Verily, verily, I say unto thee, Except a man be born of water and of the Spirit, he cannot enter into the kingdom of God.

Jesus was not speaking of a physical rebirth, but rather a spiritual rebirth. A human is both a physical and a spiritual creature. However, at the fall of man, his spiritual nature suffered. One of my favorite authors while in seminary was Charles Ryrie. Writing shortly after the Second World War, he described a brick building that had been bombed. The walls were still standing but the interior of the building had collapsed into itself. Such is the case with a fallen man. Verse 6:

6 That which is born of the flesh is flesh; and that which is born of the Spirit is spirit.

We are going to stop before the next verse. It includes a pronoun that refers back to a noun mentioned in verse 1. The majority of Christians will miss this as it is rarely, if ever, taught. One of the benefits of reading the King James Bible is the differentiation of the singular and plural "you." In other languages like French, Spanish, and the original Greek, the King James include "thee" and "ye" which are singular and plural respectively. For those who find this foreign, think of "ye" as similar to the American "you all" or "y'all." Verse 7:

7 Marvel not that I said unto thee [singular], <u>Ye [plural] must be born again</u>.

Here, Jesus is speaking directly to the individual Nicodemus, but He is referring to the group of which Nicodemus is a member. Did you see it? I will get back to this shortly and let you think about it.

Jesus explains the Spirit is not seen but felt. Verses 8-10:

8 The wind bloweth where it listeth, and thou hearest the sound thereof, but

canst not tell whence [wherefrom] it cometh, and whither [where] it goeth: so is every one that is born of the Spirit.

9 Nicodemus answered and said unto him, How can these things be?

10 Jesus answered and said unto him, <u>Art thou a master of Israel, and knowest not these things?</u>

Jesus asks Nicodemus if he is not a master or ruler over Israel. In verse 1, we are told that he was one of the Pharisees who are the group of religious rulers over Israel. In the Old Testament, God judged and blessed Israel as a group based upon the actions of their leaders. Why? As a nation, they are judged as a whole; not as individuals. Unlike Israel, God will judge Gentiles individually.

Israel's immediate future depends upon their religious rulers' accepting or rejecting the Messiah. If their rulers reject their King, then the glory of Israel and the Kingdom will be delayed. Verse 11:

11 Verily, verily, I say unto thee, We speak that we do know, and testify that we have seen; and ye receive not our witness.

The ability of Israel's rulers to perform their future task is under consideration. What is this future task? Israel's destiny includes the role they will play in the future Kingdom. What is that role? Here are four verses that support the same answer.

Exodus 19:6:

> 6 And ye shall be unto me <u>a kingdom of priests</u>, and an holy nation . . .

Isaiah 61:6:

> 6 But ye shall be named the <u>Priests of the LORD</u>: men shall call you the Ministers of our God . . .

1 Peter 2:9:

> 9 But ye are a chosen generation, <u>a royal priesthood</u>, an holy nation, a peculiar people; that ye should shew forth the praises of him who hath called you out of darkness into his marvellous light:

Revelation 1:6

> 6 And hath made us <u>kings and priests unto God</u> and his Father . . .

With this knowledge, when we read the following verses, they make sense. John 3: 12-13:

12 If I have told you earthly things, and ye believe not, how shall ye believe, if I tell you of heavenly things?

13 And no man hath ascended up to heaven, but he that came down from heaven, even [that is to say] the Son of man which is in heaven.

In both the past and now in the present, God expected Israel to operate on faith. John uses the example of the people in the Wilderness. God sent serpents as a curse on the people so that they would, in faith, turn to God. The solution was looking past the serpents and following God's instructions. It was having faith in what God said that would save them. Moses made a bronze serpent and put it up on a pole. Those who, by faith, looked up at the bronze serpent as God instructed them would be saved. Verses 14-15:

14 And as Moses lifted up the serpent in the wilderness, even [that is to say] so must the Son of man be lifted up:

15 That whosoever believeth in him

should not perish, but have eternal life.

In seminary, we called this a "type." It is something in the past that represents something else in the future. Israel will need to look up at the Messiah, the Lamb of God. He will represent sin being lifted up on the Cross. Like their fathers, those who, in faith, look up at the Savior upon the Cross will live.

Remember that John wants the readers to know the Person and purpose of Jesus Christ. Here is the purpose for which God sent His Son. Verses 16-18:

> 16 **For God so loved the world, that he gave his only begotten Son, that whosoever believeth in him should not perish, but have everlasting life.**

> 17 **For God sent not his Son into the world to condemn the world; but that the world through him might be saved.**

> 18 **He that believeth on him is not condemned: but he that believeth not is condemned already, because he hath not believed in the name of the only begotten Son of God.**

Notice that John wrote, "He that believeth on him" (v.18). The pronoun "he" refers to an individual and not a group. So, an individual's salvation is dependent upon their own faith—believing God's Word. However, Israel's future as a nation is dependent upon their religious rulers.

The remainder of this chapter is devoted to making clear the importance of an individual's faith upon their salvation. The best place to do that is from the book of Hebrews. Chapter 11 provides an excellent summary of the children of Israel who exhibited exemplary faith before God! Hebrews 11:1-3:

> 1 **Now faith is the substance of things hoped for, the evidence of things not seen. 2 For by it the elders obtained a good report.**
>
> 3 **Through faith we understand that the worlds were framed by the word of God, so that things which are seen were not made of things which do appear.**

Now, the entire chapter is dedicated to making the point that it was "by faith" that all the men of God received their blessings. I recommend that you stop and read the entire chapter of Hebrews 11. However, for our purpose, I will condense into a list.

"By faith Abel offered unto God a more excellent sacrifice than Cain, by which he obtained witness that he was righteous, God testifying of his gifts: and by it he being dead yet speaketh" (v. 4).

"By faith Enoch was translated that he should not see death; and was not found, because God had translated him: for before his translation he had this testimony, that he pleased God" (v 5).

"By faith Noah, being warned of God of things not seen as yet, moved with fear, prepared an ark to the saving of his house; by the which he condemned the world, and became heir of the righteousness which is by faith" (v. 7).

"By faith Abraham, when he was called to go out into a place which he should after receive for an inheritance, obeyed; and he went out, not knowing whither he went. By faith he sojourned in the land of promise, as in a strange country, dwelling in tabernacles with Isaac and Jacob, the heirs with him of the same promise:" (v. 8-9).

"Through faith also Sara herself received strength to conceive seed, and was delivered of a child when she was past age, because she judged him faithful who had promised" (v. 11).

"By faith Abraham, when he was tried, offered up Isaac: and he that had received the promises offered up his only begotten son, Of whom it was said, That in Isaac shall thy seed be called: Accounting that God was able to raise him up, even from the dead; from whence also he received him in a figure" (v.17-19).

"By faith Isaac blessed Jacob and Esau concerning things to come" (v. 20).

" By faith Jacob, when he was a dying, blessed both the sons of Joseph; and worshipped, leaning upon the top of his staff" (v.21).

" By faith Joseph, when he died, made mention of the departing of the children of Israel; and gave commandment concerning his bones" (v.22).

"By faith Moses, when he was born, was hid three months of his parents, because they saw he was a proper child; and they were not afraid of the king's commandment.

"By faith Moses, when he was come to years, refused to be called the son of Pharaoh's daughter;" (v. 24).

"By faith the harlot Rahab perished not with them that believed not, when she had received the spies with peace" (v. 31).

The above verses support the point that John makes concerning God and the faith. Do not miss the blessing. Read Hebrews 11. The writer of Hebrews makes two important points. Hebrews 11:6:

> 6 But <u>without faith it is impossible to please him</u>: for he that cometh to God must believe that he is, and that he is a rewarder of them that diligently seek him.

The other point comes at the close of the chapter where he summarizes. Hebrews 11:39-40:

> 39 And these all, having obtained a good report through faith, received not the promise: 40 <u>God having provided some better thing for us</u>, that they without us should not be made perfect.

The people of faith listed above died believing and not having received. Yet, the people now have something better. They have in their midst the Son of God confirming the promises made to the fathers. (See Romans 15:8.)

5

John 3 (Part II)

In the previous chapter, the Apostle John made an important point for the Jews. Jesus Christ is the Messiah and the Son of God. They are to acknowledge these facts are true and believe them. It is the basis of their salvation—faith in God. John 3:19-21:

19 **And this is the condemnation, that light is come into the world, and men loved darkness rather than light, because their deeds were evil.**

20 **For every one that doeth evil hateth the light, neither cometh to the light, lest his deeds should be reproved.**

21 **But he that doeth truth cometh to the light, that his deeds may be made manifest [known], that they are wrought in**

God.

John compares this knowledge of the truth with the coming of the light. Isaiah 9:2:

> 2 **The people that walked in darkness have seen a great light: they that dwell in the land of the shadow of death, upon them hath the light shined.**

There was an urgent need for the light to come upon Israel. John 3:22-24:

> 22 **After these things came Jesus and his disciples into the land of Judaea; and there he tarried with them, and baptized.**

> 23 **And John also was baptizing in Aenon near to Salim, because there was much water there: and they came, and were baptized.** 24 **For John was not yet cast into prison.**

It was common for each teacher to have followers who are referred to as disciples. They are students because they are learning the teaching or discipline of this teacher. This applied to John the Baptist whose disciples came to report that Jesus was baptizing also. Perhaps, they saw this as competition, but their teacher puts this to rest. Verses 25-29:

25 Then there arose a question between some of John's disciples and the Jews about purifying.

26 And they came unto John, and said unto him, Rabbi, he that was with thee beyond Jordan, to whom thou barest witness, behold, the same baptizeth, and all men come to him.

27 John answered and said, A man can receive nothing, except it be given [to] him from heaven.

28 Ye yourselves bear me witness, that I said, I am not the Christ, but that I am sent before him.

29 He that hath the bride is the bridegroom: but the friend of the bridegroom, which standeth and heareth him, rejoiceth greatly because of the bridegroom's voice: this my joy therefore is fulfilled.

In proclaiming repentance and baptism, John

the Baptist was fulfilling his role. He came to announce the arrival of the Messiah and the Son of God.

John the Baptist is speaking about Jesus as the Messiah Who has now come. Verses 30-31:

> 30 **He must increase, but I must decrease.**

> 31 **He that cometh from above is above all: he that is of the earth is earthly, and speaketh of the earth: he that cometh from heaven is above all.**

Notice what John the Baptist says about faith. Jesus is bringing a message from His Father. If someone hears and receives His testimony, they "set their seal" or agree that what He said is true. They believe. They have faith in His Word. Verses 32-33:

> 32 **And what he hath seen and heard, that he testifieth; and no man receiveth his testimony.**

> 33 **He that hath received his testimony hath set to his seal that God is true.**

Below the word "measure" means "a portion." John says that Jesus was not given a "portion" of the Spirit, but He was given all things. Verses 34-35:

34 For he whom God hath sent speaketh the words of God: for God giveth not the Spirit by measure unto him.

35 <u>The Father loveth the Son, and hath given all things into his hand.</u>

This has been all about Israel's faith and all about the children of Abraham. Nothing here has to do with the Gentiles. To learn more about God's plan for the nations, read *The Hidden Gospel.* For a more advanced approach, consider reading *Letters To Theophilus.*

The Apostle John concludes with an emphasis on believing and noting that there are eternal consequences. Their faith must be based upon Jesus, their Messiah and the Son of God. Verse 36:

36 <u>He that believeth on the Son hath everlasting life</u>: and <u>he that believeth not the Son shall not see life;</u> but the wrath of God abideth on him.

6

John 4

In Jesus' early ministry, He spent much of His time around the Sea of Galilee and surrounding towns. The Pharisees and religious rulers of Jerusalem would eventually present increasing opposition, ultimately leading to His death. John 4:1-3:

1 When therefore the Lord knew how the Pharisees had heard that Jesus made and baptized more disciples than John,

2 (Though Jesus himself baptized not, but his disciples,) 3 He left Judaea, and departed again into Galilee.

A brief history of the breaking up of the twelve tribes of Israel will provide a deeper understanding of our text. Following the death of King Solomon, King David's successor, Solomon's two sons divided the people of Israel into the Northern Kingdom of ten tribes and the Southern Kingdom of two tribes. The Northern Kingdom retained the name Israel. The Southern Kingdom was named Judah as it contained Judah and Benjamin. When we see the Bible refer to Israel and Judah, it is referring to the Twelve tribes collectively. In 720 BC, after repeated warnings, God allowed the Assyrian Empire to conquer and subdue the Northern Kingdom. The capital of the former Northern Kingdom was Samaria. Jerusalem was the capital of the Southern Kingdom.

The Assyrians were very clever. Instead of making their captives into slaves, they used assimilation in which they forced intermarriage. They forced the Jews to become part of their heathen nation. For this reason, the Samaritans were considered to be half-breeds. As such, the most devout Jews would avoid them. Jesus is about to travel through this region and, while there, He will interact with a Samaritan woman at the well. Verses 4-6:

> 4 **And he must needs go through Samaria. 5 Then cometh he to a city of Samaria, which is called Sychar, near to the parcel of ground that Jacob gave to his son Joseph.**
>
> 6 **Now Jacob's well was there. Jesus**

therefore, being wearied with his journey, sat thus on the well: and it was about the sixth hour.

The sixth hour of the day would be noontime, in the heat of the day. As most travelers begin their journey in the cool of the morning, Jesus had no doubt been walking for some time. It would be unheard of for a Jewish man to have a conversation with a Samaritan woman. Verses 7-12:

7 There cometh a woman of Samaria to draw water: Jesus saith unto her, Give me to drink. 8 (For his disciples were gone away unto the city to buy meat.)

9 Then saith the woman of Samaria unto him, How is it that thou, being a Jew, askest drink of me, which am a woman of Samaria? for the Jews have no dealings with the Samaritans.

10 Jesus answered and said unto her, If thou knewest the gift of God, and who it is that saith to thee, Give me to drink; thou wouldest have asked of him, and he would have given thee living water.

11 The woman saith unto him, Sir, thou

hast nothing to draw with, and the well is deep: from whence then hast thou that living water?

12 Art thou greater than our father Jacob, which gave us the well, and drank thereof himself, and his children, and his cattle?

Samaritans still consider Jacob, who is also called Israel, to be their father. Their conversation continues. Verses 13-14:

13 Jesus answered and said unto her, Whosoever drinketh of this water shall thirst again:

14 But whosoever drinketh of the water that I shall give him shall never thirst; but the water that I shall give him shall be in him a well of water springing up into everlasting life.

Jesus is speaking about spiritual water. Daily this woman came to the well to draw water. So, she is interested in this living water. Verse 15:

15 The woman saith unto him, Sir, give me this water, that I thirst not, neither

come hither [here] to draw.

As the Son of God, Jesus knows all about her life. Verses 16-18:

16 Jesus saith unto her, Go, call thy husband, and come hither.

17 The woman answered and said, I have no husband. Jesus said unto her, Thou hast well said, I have no husband:

18 For thou hast had five husbands; and he whom thou now hast is not thy husband: in that saidst thou truly.

The Samaritans still consider themselves to be children of Abraham although they have intermixed with Gentiles. There are many Jews today who find that this also applies to them. They continue their dialog. Verses 19-22:

19 The woman saith unto him, Sir, I perceive that thou art a prophet. 20 Our fathers worshipped in this mountain; and ye say, that in Jerusalem is the place where men ought to worship.

21 Jesus saith unto her, Woman, believe

me, the hour cometh, when ye shall neither in this mountain, nor yet at Jerusalem, worship the Father.

22 <u>Ye worship ye know not what: we [Jews] know what we worship: for salvation is of the Jews.</u>

The Samaritans do not know what they worship, but the Jews know. Is there not an exclusivity concerning salvation as it relates to the Jews alone?

During the time of Jesus' earthly ministry, the Gospel of the Kingdom was directed "unto the lost sheep of the house of Israel" (Matt. 15:24). Are not the Samaritans children of Abraham and children of Jacob also? We will see how Jesus responds to the Samaritans shortly. With the arrival of the Son of God, it is no longer about the place of worship, but rather the object of worship. Here we find our answer to the question concerning the exclusivity of salvation to the Jews. John 4: 23-26:

23 But the hour cometh, and now is, when the true worshippers shall worship the Father in spirit and in truth: for the Father seeketh such to worship him.

24 God is a Spirit: and they that worship

him must worship him in spirit and in truth.

25 The woman saith unto him, I know that Messiah cometh, which is called Christ: when he is come, he will tell us all things. 26 Jesus saith unto her, <u>I that speak unto thee am he.</u>

The title "Christ" comes from the Greek word "*Christos*" meaning "Anointed One." Notice that she is aware of the promises made through the prophets.

Their conversation drew to an end as the disciples returned from obtaining food. Notice the surprise amongst the disciples that Jesus was speaking with a woman! Verses 27-34:

27 And upon this came his disciples, and marvelled that he talked with the woman: yet no man said, What seekest thou? or, Why talkest thou with her?

28 The woman then left her waterpot, and went her way into the city, and saith to the men, 29 Come, see a man, which told me all things that ever I did: is not this the Christ?

30 Then they went out of the city, and came unto him. 31 In the mean while his disciples prayed [asked] him, saying, Master, eat.

32 But he said unto them, I have meat to eat that ye know not of. 33 Therefore said the disciples one to another, Hath any man brought him ought [something] to eat?

34 Jesus saith unto them, My meat is to do the will of him that sent me, and to finish his work.

Speaking of food, Jesus remarks that the harvest will be in four months. He compares a literal harvest with a spiritual harvest of believers. Verse 35:

35 Say not ye, There are yet four months, and then cometh harvest? behold, I say unto you, <u>Lift up your eyes, and look on the fields; for they are white already to harvest.</u>

Those who are workers in the field will receive the benefits or blessings of everlasting life. Verses 36-38:

36 And he that reapeth receiveth wages,

and gathereth fruit unto life eternal: that both he that soweth and he that reapeth may rejoice together.

37 And herein is that saying true, One soweth, and another reapeth.

38 I sent you to reap that whereon ye bestowed no labour: other men laboured, and ye are entered into their labours.

The conversation that Jesus had and His acceptance of this woman being a Samaritan was good news for the local people. Many came out to meet Jesus. They heard the good news of the Gospel of the Kingdom and believed. Verses 39-42:

39 And many of the Samaritans of that city believed on him for the saying of the woman, which testified, He told me all that ever I did.

40 So when the Samaritans were come unto him, they besought him that he would tarry [stay] with them: and he abode there two days.

41 And many more believed because of his own word;

42 And said unto the woman, Now we believe, not because of thy saying: for we have heard him ourselves, and know that this is indeed the Christ, the Saviour of the world.

These Samaritans, marginalized by the religious leaders and righteous Jews, were welcomed by the Messiah. As such, they heard, believed, and were saved by their faith.

He cared enough about these Samaritans to remain with them before continuing on His way to Galilee. Verses 43-47:

43 Now after two days he departed thence, and went into Galilee. **44** For Jesus himself testified, that a prophet hath no honour in his own country.

45 Then when he was come into Galilee, the Galilaeans received him, having seen all the things that he did at Jerusalem at the feast: for they also went unto the feast.

46 So Jesus came again into Cana of Galilee, where he made the water wine. And there was a certain nobleman, whose son was sick at Capernaum.

47 When he heard that Jesus was come out of Judaea into Galilee, he went unto him, and besought him that he would come down, and heal his son: for he was at the point of death.

Previously, I mentioned that Israel expected God to validate His prophets by miracles, signs, and wonders. They expected no less from Jesus and, as He did these miracles, His fame spread and more people came to see Him. There would be a few who would simply have faith based upon what Jesus said, but the others required proof. Verses 48-54:

48 Then said Jesus unto him, Except ye see signs and wonders, ye will not believe.

49 The nobleman saith unto him, Sir, come down ere [before] my child die. 50 Jesus saith unto him, Go thy way; thy son liveth. And the man believed the word that Jesus had spoken unto him, and he went his way.

51 And as he was now going down, his servants met him, and told him, saying,

Thy son liveth.

52 Then enquired he of them the hour when he began to amend [heal]. And they said unto him, Yesterday at the seventh hour the fever left him.

53 So the father knew that it was at the same hour, in the which Jesus said unto him, Thy son liveth: and [he] himself believed, and his whole house.

54 This is again the second miracle that Jesus did, when he was come out of Judaea into Galilee.

7

John 5

Jesus and the disciples travel to Jerusalem for a holy day. There was a place near the Sheep Gate called the Pool of Bethesda. This pool was known to have miraculous powers which were restorative in nature. There, large crowds would gather in hopes that they may enter into the waters and be healed. John 5:1-4:

1 **After this there was a feast of the Jews; and Jesus went up to Jerusalem.**

2 **Now there is at Jerusalem by the sheep market a pool, which is called in the Hebrew tongue Bethesda, having five porches.**

3 **In these lay a great multitude of impotent folk, of blind, halt, withered, wait-**

ing for the moving of the water.

4 For an angel went down at a certain season into the pool, and troubled the water: whosoever then first after the troubling of the water stepped in was made whole of whatsoever disease he had.

The narrative focuses on a particular man who, due to his infirmities, was unable to enter the waters before the opportunity was lost. Verses 5-9:

5 And a certain man was there, which had an infirmity thirty and eight years.

6 When Jesus saw him lie, and knew that he had been now a long time in that case, he saith unto him, Wilt thou be made whole?

7 The impotent man answered him, Sir, I have no man, when the water is troubled, to put me into the pool: but while I am coming, another steppeth down before me.

8 Jesus saith unto him, Rise, take up thy bed, and walk.

9 And immediately the man was made whole, and took up his bed, and walked: and on the same day was the sabbath.

This happened in Jerusalem during the holiday and the city was crowded. There were religious leaders who always were watching. Verses 10-16:

10 The Jews therefore said unto him that was cured, It is the sabbath day: it is not lawful for thee to carry thy bed.

11 He answered them, He that made me whole, the same said unto me, Take up thy bed, and walk.

12 Then asked they him, What man is that which said unto thee, Take up thy bed, and walk? 13 And he that was healed wist [knew] not who it was: for Jesus had conveyed himself away, a multitude being in that place.

14 Afterward Jesus findeth him in the temple, and said unto him, Behold, thou art made whole: sin no more, lest a worse thing come unto thee.

15 The man departed, and told the Jews that it was Jesus, which had made him whole.

16 <u>And therefore did the Jews persecute Jesus, and sought to slay him, because he had done these things on the sabbath day</u>.

Jesus tried to avoid Jerusalem. Why? I like to explain that Jerusalem was where the hornets' nest was located.

The religious leaders found Jesus and interrogated Him. Verses 17-18:

17 But Jesus answered them, My Father worketh hitherto, and I work.

18 Therefore the Jews sought the more to kill him, because he not only had broken the sabbath, but said also that God was his Father, making himself equal with God.

Did you notice that being the Son of God makes Jesus equal to God? Verses 19-20:

19 Then answered Jesus and said unto

them, Verily, verily, I say unto you, The Son can do nothing of himself, but what he seeth the Father do: for what things soever he doeth, these also doeth the Son likewise.

20 For the Father loveth the Son, and sheweth him all things that himself doeth: and he will shew him greater works than these, that ye may marvel.

Jesus discloses the role of the Son. What the Father can do, the Son can also do. However, the Father has committed to the Son the prerogative of judgment. Jesus will be the only One to judge the living and the dead. I would think that the religious leaders would tremble with fear. Verses 21-23:

21 For as the Father raiseth up the dead, and quickeneth [makes alive] them; even so the Son quickeneth [makes alive] whom he will.

22 **For the Father judgeth no man, but hath committed all judgment unto the Son:**

23 That all men should honour the Son, even as they honour the Father. He that

honoureth not the Son honoureth not
the Father which hath sent him.

Jesus publicly proclaims that salvation for the
Jews is based upon faith. Notice His explanation of
faith. They must believe both Jesus and the One Who
sent Him. How many there do you think heard and
understood this? If you are Jewish and wish to be
saved by the Gospel of the Kingdom, then remember
this. Verses 24-27:

24 Verily, verily, I say unto you, <u>He that
heareth my word, and believeth on him
that sent me, hath everlasting life</u>, and
shall not come into condemnation; but
is passed from death unto life.

25 Verily, verily, I say unto you, The
hour is coming, and now is, when the
dead shall hear the voice of the Son of
God: and they that hear shall live.

26 For as the Father hath life in himself;
so hath he given to the Son to have life
in himself;

27 And hath given him authority to execute judgment also, because he is the
Son of man.

In the following, Jesus speaks about the resurrection. We see from the text that both the good and the evil shall be resurrected. It is not the resurrection, but the destination that should concern them. Some will have eternal life while others will have eternal damnation. Verses 28-31:

> 28 **Marvel not at this: for the hour is coming, in the which all that are in the graves shall hear his voice,**
>
> 29 **And shall come forth; they that have done good, unto the resurrection of life; and they that have done evil, unto the resurrection of damnation.**
>
> 30 **I can of mine own self do nothing: as I hear, I judge: and my judgment is just; because I seek not mine own will, but the will of the Father which hath sent me.**
>
> 31 **If I bear witness of myself, my witness is not true.**

Yes, Jesus Himself bears witness that all of this is true, but we are reminded of another witness which God sent. John the Baptist testified on Jesus' behalf. He was "the voice of him that crieth in the wilderness, Prepare ye the way of the LORD" (Isa. 40:3). Consider also Isaiah 40:5:

> 5 And <u>the glory of the LORD shall be revealed, and all flesh shall see it together</u>: for the mouth of the LORD hath spoken it.

Let us continue with our text. John 5:32-35:

> 32 There is another that beareth witness of me; and I know that the witness which he witnesseth of me is true.

> 33 Ye sent unto John, and he bare witness unto the truth. 34 But I receive not testimony from man: but these things I say, that ye might be saved.

> 35 He was a burning and a shining light: and ye were willing for a season to rejoice in his light.

There is another Witness Who testifies to the truth. This Witness sees all things. It is God the Father. He confirms the works done by Jesus. Verses 36-38:

> 36 But I have [a] greater witness than

that of John: for the works which the Father hath given me to finish, the same works that I do, bear witness of me, that the Father hath sent me.

37 And the Father himself, which hath sent me, hath borne witness of me. Ye have neither heard his voice at any time, nor seen his shape.

38 And ye have not his word abiding in you: for whom he hath sent, him ye believe not.

There is one more source of testimony and that is Scripture itself. Scripture is filled with promises and prophecies concerning the Anointed One. All of them provide a preponderance of evidence concerning the Christ. Verses 39-40:

39 Search the scriptures; for in them ye think ye have eternal life: and they are they which testify of me. 40 And ye will not come to me, that ye might have life.

Jesus knows the nature of men. They will not honor Him for they do not have the love of God in them. He is speaking to the Pharisees, rulers, religious leaders, and the self-righteous. Verses 41-42:

41 I receive not honour from men. **42** But I know you, that ye have not the love of God in you.

The Father sent Him, but they do not accept His Son. In fact, they reject Him. Verse 43:

43 I am come in my Father's name, and ye receive me not: if another shall come in his own name, him ye will receive.

Notice the last part of this verse. It says that if another comes in his own name, they will accept him. Since there is no One except Jesus Who can save, He is referring to the Antichrist. They will be deceived for they desire to receive honor from men and not the honor that comes from God. Verses 44-45:

44 How can ye believe, which receive honour one of [from] another, and seek not the honour that cometh from God only?

45 Do not think that I will accuse you to the Father: there is one that accuseth you, even [that is to say] Moses, in whom ye trust.

The Law which was given to Moses will accuse them.

If they do not believe the words of Moses, then they will not believe the words of Jesus. Verses 46-47:

46 **For had ye believed Moses, ye would have believed me: for he wrote of me.**

47 **But if ye believe not his writings, how shall ye believe my words?**

8

John 6

The Sea of Galilee is in the northeastern part of present-day Israel. Jesus went there to continue His ministry. Notice that it was His miracles that attracted the people. John 6:1-4:

> 1 **After these things Jesus went over the sea of Galilee, which is the sea of Tiberias.**
>
> 2 **And a great multitude followed him, because they saw his miracles which he did on them that were diseased.**
>
> 3 **And Jesus went up into a mountain, and there he sat with his disciples.** 4 **And the passover, a feast of the Jews, was nigh.**

Jesus taught them about God and the Gospel of the Kingdom. The people sat and listened as they never heard someone teach with such authority.

It would soon be evening. The multitude of people had no food and were far from any town. Verses 5-10:

> 5 When Jesus then lifted up his eyes, and saw a great company come unto him, he saith unto Philip, Whence shall we buy bread, that these may eat? 6 And this he said to prove [test] him: for he himself knew what he would do.

> 7 Philip answered him, Two hundred pennyworth of bread is not sufficient for them, that every one of them may take a little.

> 8 One of his disciples, Andrew, Simon Peter's brother, saith unto him, 9 There is a lad here, which hath five barley loaves, and two small fishes: but what are they among so many?

> 10 And Jesus said, Make the men sit down. Now there was much grass in the place. So the men sat down, in number

about five thousand.

It was common to number a crowd by counting the adult men only. To this number, we must add the women and children. Notice that they ate and were all filled. Verses 11-14:

11 **And Jesus took the loaves; and when he had given thanks, he distributed to the disciples, and the disciples to them that were set down; and likewise of the fishes as much as they would.**

12 **When they were filled, he said unto his disciples, Gather up the fragments that remain, that nothing be lost.**

13 **Therefore they gathered them together, and filled twelve baskets with the fragments of the five barley loaves, which remained over and above unto them that had eaten.**

14 **Then those men, when they had seen the miracle that Jesus did, said, This is of a truth that prophet that should come into the world.**

Because of this miracle, the men there believed that

Jesus was a prophet and that He spoke the words of God.

Since Jesus met their physical need for food, many of them wanted to make Him their king. Yet, there is no indication that they knew Jesus is the Messiah and the Son of God. Verse 15:

> **15 When Jesus therefore perceived that they would come and take him by force, to make him a king, he departed again into a mountain himself alone.**

Evening came. They had spent the day beside the sea and a ship awaited. In Matthew, we are told that Jesus chose to remain to dismiss the people while the disciples departed for their next destination. Jesus told them He would meet them there as He desired to be alone. (See Matthew 14:22-23.) Verses 16-17:

> **16 And when even was now come, his disciples went down unto the sea, 17 And entered into a ship, and went over the sea toward Capernaum. And it was now dark, and Jesus was not come to them.**

The winds on the Sea of Galilee can become violent. While in this ship, a storm arose. Verses 18-19:

18 And the sea arose by reason of a great wind that blew. 19 So when they had rowed about five and twenty or thirty furlongs, they see Jesus walking on the sea, and drawing nigh unto the ship: and they were afraid.

They were between two to three miles from shore when they saw what appeared to be an apparition. They were filled with fear until Jesus spoke to them. Verses 20-21:

20 But he saith unto them, It is I; be not afraid. 21 Then they willingly received him into the ship: and immediately the ship was at the land whither they went.

Other boats came to where Jesus and the disciples had fed the multitude looking to find Him. Not finding Him, they took their boats to Capernaum to look there. Verses 22-24:

22 The day following, when the people which stood on the other side of the sea saw that there was none other boat there, save that one whereinto his disciples were entered, and that Jesus went not with his disciples into the boat, but that his disciples were gone away alone;

23 (Howbeit there came other boats from Tiberias nigh unto the place where they did eat bread, after that the Lord had given thanks:)

24 When the people therefore saw that Jesus was not there, neither his disciples, they also took shipping, and came to Capernaum, seeking for Jesus.

Jesus knew why they sought Him. It was for the sake of their stomachs. I picture Jesus on another shore and the passengers of these boats coming to Him. Verses 25-26:

25 And when they had found him on the other side of the sea, they said unto him, Rabbi, when camest thou hither?

26 Jesus answered them and said, Verily, verily, I say unto you, Ye seek me, not because ye saw the miracles, but because ye did eat of the loaves, and were filled.

Jesus teaches them about the food they should be seeking. Verse 27:

27 Labour not for the meat which per-

isheth, but for that meat which en-
dureth unto everlasting life, which the
Son of man shall give unto you: for him
hath God the Father sealed.

This becomes a dialog between Jesus and the
people on the shore. Verses 28-35:

28 Then said they unto him, What shall
we do, that we might work the works of
God? 29 Jesus answered and said unto
them, This is the work of God, that ye
believe on him whom he hath sent.

30 They said therefore unto him, What
sign shewest thou then, that we may
see, and believe thee? what dost thou
work? 31 Our fathers did eat manna in
the desert; as it is written, He gave them
bread from heaven to eat.

32 Then Jesus said unto them, Verily,
verily, I say unto you, Moses gave you
not that bread from heaven; but my Father giveth you the true bread from
heaven. 33 For the bread of God is he
which cometh down from heaven, and
giveth life unto the world.

34 Then said they unto him, Lord, evermore give us this bread. **35** And Jesus said unto them, I am the bread of life: he that cometh to me shall never hunger; and he that believeth on me shall never thirst.

In Jesus' conversation with the Samaritan woman at the well, He compared Himself to living water. Here, He compares Himself to the bread of life. He is speaking to their basic needs for life.

It is clear that they do not know Who Jesus is. We will pause here to discuss the three offices or roles of the Messiah. His first role is that of Prophet. Yes, He is the Son of God, but the office He is exercising during His earthly ministry is that of Prophet. He came to speak the words that the Father gives Him; not His own words. Remember this as we continue shortly. The second role or office of the Messiah is that of Priest. Once He has ascended into heaven, the Father will appoint Him as Priest to intercede on behalf of Israel. Finally, His third office is that of King. Jesus will return as King to avenge the enemies of His people. Then, He will establish His eternal Kingdom promised to King David. Again, while on earth, He acts as a Prophet.

All that has been written about Jesus, according to prophecy, will happen. Verses 36-38:

> 36 But I said unto you, That ye also have seen me, and believe not. 37 All that the Father giveth me shall come to me; and him that cometh to me I will in no wise cast out.

> 38 For I came down from heaven, not to do mine own will, but the will of him that sent me.

God sent Jesus to reclaim that which was lost. Jesus stated, "I am not sent but unto the lost sheep of the house of Israel" (Matt. 15:24). He came to confirm the promises made to the fathers: Abraham, Isaac, and Jacob. (See Romans 15:9.) Verses 39-40:

> 39 And this is the Father's will which hath sent me, that of all which he hath given me I should lose nothing, but should raise it up again at the last day.

> 40 And this is the will of him that sent me, that every one which seeth the Son, and believeth on him, may have everlasting life: and I will raise him up at the last day.

Those who believe and have faith in Jesus as their Messiah and the Son of God, will have everlasting life because of Him.

Some of those in the crowd knew Jesus from His youth. They muttered to themselves about Him and what He said. Verses 41-44:

> 41 The Jews then murmured at him, because he said, I am the bread which came down from heaven.
>
> 42 And they said, Is not this Jesus, the son of Joseph, whose father and mother we know? how is it then that he saith, I came down from heaven?
>
> 43 Jesus therefore answered and said unto them, Murmur not among yourselves. 44 No man can come to me, except the Father which hath sent me draw him: and I will raise him up at the last day.

Jesus asked His disciples, "But whom say ye that I am?" (Matt. 16:15). To this, Peter responded, " Thou art the Christ, the Son of the living God" (v. 16). Notice how Jesus responded to Peter's statement. Matthew 16:17:

17 And Jesus answered and said unto him, Blessed art thou, Simon Barjona: <u>for flesh and blood hath not revealed it unto thee, but my Father which is in heaven.</u>

There is a unique relationship between God and His chosen people Israel. He would nurture and teach them as His children. John 6:45-47:

45 It is written in the prophets, And they shall be all taught of [by] God. Every man therefore that hath heard, and hath learned of [by] the Father, cometh unto me.

46 Not that any man hath seen the Father, save [except] he which is of God, he hath seen the Father. 47 Verily, verily, I say unto you, <u>He that believeth on me hath everlasting life.</u>

Like their father Abraham, their relationship with God is one based upon faith, believing His Word, and trusting Him.

Jesus returns to comparing Himself to the "bread of life." He makes a comparison to the Wilderness where the Jews were totally dependent upon

God. He even uses the name "I am." Verses 48-49:

> 48 <u>I am</u> **that bread of life.** 49 **Your fathers did eat manna in the wilderness, and are dead.**

The manna that God gave them was sustenance but not eternal life. The bread which Jesus offers, referring to Himself, will allow them to live forever. Verses 50-51:

> 50 **This is the bread which cometh down from heaven, that a man may eat thereof, and not die.**

> 51 <u>I am the living bread which came down from heaven: if any man eat of this bread, he shall live for ever</u>: **and the bread that I will give is my flesh, which I will give for the life of the world.**

What was the reaction of the Jews who heard Him? The word "stove" means "struggled in opposition to each other; contented or disputed." Verse 52:

> 52 **The Jews therefore strove among themselves, saying, How can this man give us his flesh to eat?**

Did they not eat the flesh of the Passover Lamb? Did they not place its blood on their doorways? Here, Jesus is not referring to actually eating His flesh or drinking His blood. Rather, it is symbolic in the elements of communion. If you are Jewish, consider the fifth glass of wine reserved for Elijah. No one drinks from that cup during the Passover Seder. It is reserved for the prophet's return. That cup represents the blood of the New Covenant and symbolizes the sacrifice of Yeshua HaMashiach. The New Covenant was foretold by the Prophet Jeremiah. God will write the Law upon their hearts. (See Jeremiah 31:31-33.) For a detailed explanation, read *The Glorious Destiny of Israel: The Fulfillment of G-d's Promises and Prophecies to Israel.*

Jesus is speaking about His body and His blood to be sacrificed for them. It is part of the Passover meal and is symbolic. Verses 53-56:

53 **Then Jesus said unto them, Verily, verily, I say unto you, Except ye eat the flesh of the Son of man, and drink his blood, ye have no life in you.**

54 **Whoso eateth my flesh, and drinketh my blood, hath eternal life; and I will raise him up at the last day.** 55 **For my flesh is meat indeed, and my blood is**

drink indeed. 56 He that eateth my flesh,
and drinketh my blood, dwelleth in me,
and I in him.

God sent His Son for this purpose. Jesus tells
them about His coming death in which He takes
upon Himself the sin of the world. He is their Passover Lamb. Verses 57-58:

57 As the living Father hath sent me, and
I live by the Father: so he that eateth me,
even he shall live by me.

58 This is that bread which came down
from heaven: not as your fathers did eat
manna, and are dead: he that eateth of
this bread shall live for ever.

There can be no misunderstanding. This message was specifically intended for the children of
Abraham; not the Gentiles. He was teaching the Jews
in a synagogue. Yet, as you would expect, His message offended those who heard it. Verses 59-61:

59 These things said he in the synagogue, as he taught in Capernaum.

60 Many therefore of his disciples, when
they had heard this, said, This is an hard

saying; who can hear it? 61 When Jesus knew in himself that his disciples murmured at it, he said unto them, Doth this offend you?

Jesus speaks to His disciples. They also murmured. He asks them a question alluding to His Ascension. Later, after His resurrection, Jesus would be taken up into heaven. Verses 62-65:

62 What and if ye shall see the Son of man ascend up where he was before?

63 It is the spirit that quickeneth; the flesh profiteth nothing: the words that I speak unto you, they are spirit, and they are life.

64 But there are some of you that believe not. For Jesus knew from the beginning who they were that believed not, and who should betray him.

65 And he said, Therefore said I unto you, that no man can come unto me, except it were given unto him of [by] my Father.

All of those who followed Jesus as their teacher

were called a disciple; not just the Twelve. This was a pill too bitter for some to swallow. For many, this became their point of decision. Verses 66-68:

> 66 From that time many of his disciples went back, and walked no more with him.
>
> 67 Then said Jesus unto the twelve, Will ye also go away? 68 Then Simon Peter answered him, Lord, to whom shall we go? thou hast the words of eternal life.

Peter understood and, speaking for himself and the others, he continued. Verse 69:

> 69 And we believe and are sure that thou art that Christ, the Son of the living God.

God calls those who would believe, but it is always by freewill that they choose to stay or to go. Verses 70-71.

> 70 Jesus answered them, Have not I chosen you twelve, and one of you is a devil? 71 He spake of Judas Iscariot the son of Simon: for he it was that should betray him, being one of the twelve.

9

John 7

Throughout Jesus' early ministry, He avoided Jerusalem. The reason was that He offended the established religious leaders and they wanted to kill him. In the following verse, the word "Jewry" refers to Judea which is the region where Jerusalem is located. It is here that the Chief Priest and Pharisees lived. John 7:1-3:

> 1 **After these things Jesus walked in Galilee: for he would not walk in Jewry, because the Jews sought to kill him.**
>
> 2 **Now the Jews' feast of tabernacles was at hand. 3 His brethren therefore said unto him, Depart hence, and go into Judaea, that thy disciples also may see the works that thou doest.**

His brethren wanted Jesus to go throughout Judea and make Himself known. In other words, they felt that He should promote Himself in a more populated region. For even His own brethren did not believe in Him. Verses 4-5:

> 4 For there is no man that doeth any thing in secret, and he himself seeketh to be known openly. If thou do these things, shew thyself to the world. 5 For neither did his brethren believe in him.

Jesus was aware of what would eventually happen. He had work to complete and sought to finish that work before going to Jerusalem. Verses 6-9:

> 6 Then Jesus said unto them, My time is not yet come: but your time is alway ready. 7 The world cannot hate you; but me it hateth, because I testify of it, that the works thereof are evil.

> 8 Go ye up unto this feast: I go not up yet unto this feast; for my time is not yet full come.

> 9 When he had said these words unto them, he abode still [remained] in Galilee.

Jesus stayed in Galilee while His brethren went to Jerusalem. Jesus followed alone and unnoticed. Verses 10-13:

> 10 **But when his brethren were gone up, then went he also up unto the feast, not openly, but as it were in secret.**

> 11 **Then the Jews sought him at the feast, and said, Where is he?** 12 **And there was much murmuring among the people concerning him: for some said, He is a good man: others said, Nay; but he deceiveth the people.**

> 13 **Howbeit no man spake openly of him for fear of the Jews.**

Jesus arrived after the feast started.

Jesus' knowledge of Scripture was superior to any of the degreed Pharisees. Verses 14-15:

> 14 **Now about the midst of the feast Jesus went up into the temple, and taught.**

> 15 **And the Jews marvelled, saying, How knoweth this man letters, having never learned?**

He debates with them in the Temple. However, He knows their thoughts. Verses 16-19:

> 16 Jesus answered them, and said, My doctrine is not mine, but his that sent me. 17 If any man will do his will, he shall know of the doctrine, whether it be of God, or whether I speak of myself.

> 18 He that speaketh of himself seeketh his own glory: but he that seeketh his glory that sent him, the same is true, and no unrighteousness is in him.

> 19 Did not Moses give you the law, and yet none of you keepeth the law? Why go ye about to kill me?

They are still offended that He healed the man at the Pool of Bethesda on the sabbath! Verses 20-31:

> 20 The people answered and said, Thou hast a devil: who goeth about to kill thee? 21 Jesus answered and said unto them, I have done one work, and ye all marvel.

> 22 Moses therefore gave unto you circumcision; (not because it is of Moses,

but of the fathers;) and ye on the sabbath day circumcise a man.

23 If a man on the sabbath day receive circumcision, that the law of Moses should not be broken; are ye angry at me, because I have made a man every whit [bit] whole on the sabbath day?

24 Judge not according to the appearance, but judge [with a] righteous judgment. 25 Then said some of them of Jerusalem, Is not this he, whom they seek to kill?

26 But, lo, he speaketh boldly, and they say nothing unto him. Do the rulers know indeed that this is the very Christ [Anointed One]? 27 Howbeit we know this man whence [wherefrom] he is: but when Christ cometh, no man knoweth whence [wherefrom] he is.

28 Then cried Jesus in the temple as he taught, saying, Ye both know me, and ye know whence [wherefrom] I am: and I am not come of myself, but he that sent me is true, whom ye know not.

29 But I know him: for I am from him, and he hath sent me.

30 Then they sought to take him: but no man laid hands on him, because his hour was not yet come.

31 And <u>many of the people believed on him</u>, and said, <u>When Christ cometh, will he do more miracles than these which this man hath done?</u>

If Jesus had gone to Jerusalem with His disciples, then He might not have made it to the Temple before they took Him.

Jesus taught the people as One with authority. This angered the Pharisees and chief priests. Jesus would only be with them a short time longer. Then, they will not be able to find Him. He was speaking about His Ascension. Verses 32-34:

32 The Pharisees heard that the people murmured such things concerning him; and the Pharisees and the chief priests sent officers to take him.

33 Then said Jesus unto them, Yet a little while am I with you, and then I go unto

him that sent me. 34 Ye shall seek me, and shall not find me: and where I am, thither [there] ye cannot come.

When the Jews were forced to leave their homes due to invasions and persecutions, it was referred to as the dispersion. Another name for this is the Diaspora. Consider a dandelion that is white with seeds. Children put it to their mouth and blow on it. All the seeds are scattered. It was like this for the Jews. They were scattered among the nations. They will remain scattered until they are called to return to the Promised Land. Verses 35-39:

35 Then said the Jews among themselves, Whither will he go, that we shall not find him? will he go unto the dispersed among the Gentiles, and teach the Gentiles?

36 What manner of saying is this that he said, Ye shall seek me, and shall not find me: and where I am, thither ye cannot come?

37 In the last day, that great day of the feast, Jesus stood and cried, saying, If any man thirst, let him come unto me, and drink.

38 He that believeth on me, as the scripture hath said, out of his belly shall flow rivers of living water.

39 (But this spake he of the Spirit, which they that believe on him should receive: for the Holy Ghost was not yet given; because that Jesus was not yet glorified.)

On that day at the Temple, numerous Jews believed that what He said was true. That is the faith that saves! Verses 40-44:

40 Many of the people therefore, when they heard this saying, said, Of a truth this is the Prophet.

41 Others said, This is the Christ. But some said, Shall Christ come out of Galilee? 42 Hath not the scripture said, That Christ cometh of the seed of David, and out of the town of Bethlehem, where David was?

43 So there was a division among the people because of him. 44 And some of them would have taken him; but no man laid hands on him.

Let us pause for a moment to discuss the objection raised, "Hath not the scripture said, That Christ cometh of the seed of David" (v. 42). We have proof that Jesus met the criteria established by the prophets. In the opening verses of the Gospel of Matthew, the first book following the end of the Old Testament, provides the evidence. There, we find the lengthy geneaology of Jesus. Notice how the geneaology begins. Matthew 1:1:

> 1 **The book of the generation of Jesus Christ, <u>the son of David, the son of Abraham.</u>**

We must understand that this was not a last minute plan by God. It was foreordained before the foundation of the world. 1 Peter 1:19-21:

> 19 **But with the precious blood of Christ, as of a lamb without blemish and without spot:** 20 **<u>Who verily was foreordained before the foundation of the world,</u> but was manifest [made known] in these last times for you,**
>
> 21 **<u>Who by him do believe in God, that raised him up from the dead, and gave him glory; that your faith and hope might be in God.</u>**

There is that word "faith" again. Jews must place their faith and hope "in God."

The religious leaders interrogated the officers of the Temple's security guards. John 6:45-53:

> 45 Then came the officers to the chief priests and Pharisees; and they said unto them [the officers], Why have ye not brought him? 46 The officers answered, Never man spake like this man.

> 47 Then answered them the Pharisees, Are ye also deceived? 48 Have any of the rulers or of the Pharisees believed on him? 49 But this people who knoweth not the law are cursed.

> 50 Nicodemus saith unto them, (he that came to Jesus by night, being one of them,) 51 Doth our law judge any man, before it hear him, and know what he doeth?

> 52 They answered and said unto him, Art thou also of Galilee? Search, and look: for out of Galilee ariseth no prophet. 53 And every man went unto his own house.

10

John 8

The next day, Jesus went again to the Temple to teach the people. While He was teaching, the Pharisees came to test Him. John 8:1-4:

1 **Jesus went unto the mount of Olives. 2 And early in the morning he came again into the temple, and all the people came unto him; and he sat down, and taught them.**

3 **And the scribes and Pharisees brought unto him a woman taken in adultery; and when they had set her in the midst,**

4 **They say unto him, Master, this woman was taken in adultery, in the very act.**

The Pharisees tell Jesus the Law. Then, the people listen to Jesus explain the Law to those who are supposedly experts in the Law. Verses 5-8:

> 5 **Now Moses in the law commanded us, that such should be stoned: but what sayest thou?**

> 6 **This they said, tempting [testing] him, that they might have to accuse him. But Jesus stooped down, and with his finger wrote on the ground, as though he heard them not.**

> 7 **So when they continued asking him, he lifted up himself, and said unto them, He that is without sin among you, let him first cast a stone at her.**

> 8 **And again he stooped down, and wrote on the ground.**

Like an attorney doodling on his legal pad, Jesus was letting all of them think about what He had said. As they thought about it, each left convicted of their own sin. Verse 9:

> 9 **And they which heard it, being convicted by their own conscience, went**

out one by one, beginning at the eldest, even unto the last: and Jesus was left alone, and the woman standing in the midst.

At this point, Jesus stands up. He and the woman face each other. Consider their conversation. Verses 10-11:

10 When Jesus had lifted up himself, and saw none but the woman, he said unto her, Woman, where are those thine accusers? hath no man condemned thee?

11 She said, No man, Lord. And Jesus said unto her, Neither do I condemn thee: go, and sin no more.

After all this had happened, only the Pharisees remained. Verses 12-15:

12 Then spake Jesus again unto them, saying, I am the light of the world: he that followeth me shall not walk in darkness, but shall have the light of life.

13 The Pharisees therefore said unto him, Thou bearest record of thyself; thy

record is not true.

14 Jesus answered and said unto them, Though I bear record of myself, yet my record is true: for I know whence [wherefrom] I came, and whither I go; but ye cannot tell whence [wherefrom] I come, and whither I go.

15 Ye judge after the flesh; I judge no man.

Throughout the Gospel of John, he presents Jesus as the Saving Messiah and Son of God. Jesus will eventually judge the living and the dead. However, that time has not yet come. Concerning His present mission on earth, He says, "for I came not to judge the world, but to save the world" (Jn. 12:47).

When Jesus does take upon Himself the role of Judge, His verdicts will be true and appropriate. Verses 16-17:

16 And yet if I judge, my judgment is true: for I am not alone, but I and the Father that sent me.

17 It is also written in your law, that the testimony of two men is true.

We must not forget that the Father and Son are One. The Father sent the Son to bear witness to the people. His reference to His relationship with the Father incites the Jewish rulers. Verses 18-20:

> 18 **I am one that bear witness of myself, and the Father that sent me beareth witness of me.**

> 19 **Then said they unto him, Where is thy Father? Jesus answered, Ye neither know me, nor my Father: if ye had known me, ye should have known my Father also.**

> 20 **These words spake Jesus in the treasury, as he taught in the temple: and no man laid hands on him; for his hour was not yet come.**

The rulers have an opportunity to accept their Messiah. This opportunity will pass and they will not be afforded another. Jesus refers to going somewhere. Where is it that He will go? Psalms 110:1:

> 1 **The LORD [Elohim] said unto my Lord [Adonai], Sit thou at my right hand, until I make thine enemies thy footstool.**

We continue with our text. John 8:21-24:

21 Then said Jesus again unto them, I go my way, and ye shall seek me, and shall die in your sins: whither I go, ye cannot come.

22 Then said the Jews, Will he kill himself? because he saith, Whither I go, ye cannot come.

23 And he said unto them, Ye are from beneath; I am from above: ye are of this world; I am not of this world.

24 I said therefore unto you, that ye shall die in your sins: for if ye believe not that I am he, ye shall die in your sins.

Here we see the same theme from the beginning of the Gospel of John. It is all about faith. Look at verse 24. I paraphrase, "If you do not believe, if you have not faith that Jesus is the Messiah, then you shall die in your sins."

Their response reveals that they do not know Who Jesus is. Verse 25:

25 Then said they unto him, Who art

thou? And Jesus saith unto them, Even the same that I said unto you from the beginning.

Jesus remains true and does not change. He continues, but they still do not understand Verses 26-27:

> 26 **I have many things to say and to judge of you: but he that sent me is true; and I speak to the world those things which I have heard of [from] him.**

> 27 **They understood not that he spake to them of the Father.**

We need to consider something we previously read. John 3:14-15:

> 14 **And as Moses lifted up the serpent in the wilderness, even so must the Son of man be lifted up: 15 That whosoever believeth in him should not perish, but have eternal life.**

He refers to a test of faith given to Israel in the Wilderness. These religious leaders should know this. It is a reference to Jesus' crucifixion. John 8:28:

> 28 **Then said Jesus unto them, When ye**

have lifted up the Son of man, then shall ye know that I am he, and that I do nothing of myself; but as my Father hath taught me, I speak these things.

If Jesus does all that the Father wills, then His crucifixion is the predeterminate will of God. It was not a surprise. Satan did not win the battle. The Apostle Paul would later write about Christ's faithfulness to do God's will. Philippians 2:6-8:

6 Who, being in the form of God, thought it not robbery to be equal with God: 7 But made himself of no reputation, and took upon him the form of a servant, and was made in the likeness of men:

8 And being found in fashion as a man, he humbled himself, and became obedient unto death, even the death of the cross.

We continue with our text. John 8:29-32:

29 And he that sent me is with me: the Father hath not left me alone; for I do always those things that please him.

30 As he spake these words, many believed on him.

31 Then said Jesus to those Jews which believed on him, If ye continue in my word, then are ye my disciples indeed;

32 And ye shall know the truth, and the truth shall make you free.

Those who believe and have faith in Jesus must continue in that belief in order to remain His disciples. The Gospel of the Kingdom requires continued proof of their faith by righteous works. James writes, "But wilt thou know, O vain man, that faith without works is dead?" (Jas. 2:20). Again, he writes "For as the body without the spirit is dead, so faith without works is dead also" (Jas. 2:26). Is this the position that Jesus took during His earthly ministry? In His discussion with His disciples about the end times, Jesus said, "But he that shall endure unto the end, the same shall be saved" (Matt. 24:13). The sins of faithful Israel will be forgiven by the Messiah upon His return. For Gentiles, saved by the Gospel of Grace, this does not apply to you. It applies to the children of Abraham who follow the Gospel of the Kingdom.

There is an air of entitlement and superiority from the religious Jews. They are offended that Jesus does not recognize who they are. Verses 33-39:

> 33 They answered him, We be Abraham's seed, and were never in bondage to any man: how sayest thou, Ye shall be made free?

> 34 Jesus answered them, Verily, verily, I say unto you, Whosoever committeth sin is the servant of sin. 35 And the servant abideth not in the house for ever: but the Son abideth ever.

> 36 If the Son therefore shall make you free, ye shall be free indeed.

> 37 I know that ye are Abraham's seed; but ye seek to kill me, because my word hath no place in you.

> 38 I speak that which I have seen with my Father: and ye do that which ye have seen with your father.

> 39 They answered and said unto him, Abraham is our father. Jesus saith unto them, If ye were Abraham's children, ye would do the works of Abraham.

Abraham may have been their earthly father, their father in the flesh, but their spiritual father was Satan. Abraham did not want to kill God, yet they do. Verse 40:

> 40 **But now ye seek to kill me, a man that hath told you the truth, which I have heard of [from] God: this did not Abraham.**

Many Jews raise the objection that Jesus cannot be God as there is only One God. Verses 41-43:

> 41 **Ye do the deeds of your father. Then said they to him, We be not born of fornication; we have one Father, even God.**

> 42 **Jesus said unto them, If God were your Father, ye would love me: for I proceeded forth and came from God; neither came I of myself, but he sent me.**

> 43 **Why do ye not understand my speech? even [it is] because ye cannot hear my word.**

In the very beginning, Satan deceived Adam and Eve. They sinned because of Satan's lies forcing all mankind into bondage. Jesus came to redeem or buy back or free the people from this bondage to sin and Satan. Verses 44-47:

> **44 Ye are of your father the devil, and the lusts of your father ye will do. He was a murderer from the beginning [Creation], and abode not in the truth, because there is no truth in him. When he speaketh a lie, he speaketh of his own: for he is a liar, and the father of it.**

> **45 And because <u>I tell you the truth, ye believe me not</u>.**

> **46 Which of you convinceth me of sin? And if I say the truth, why do ye not believe me? 47 He that is of God heareth God's words: ye therefore hear them not, because ye are not of God.**

In verse 41 above, the Jews said that they were not born of fornication. Were they implying that Jesus was? For Joseph was Mary's husband but not His biological father. In the following, they accused Him of being a Samaritan, a half-breed, and possessed by a demon. They dishonor the Son of God. Verses 48-51:

> **48 Then answered the Jews, and said**

unto him, Say we not well that thou art a Samaritan, and hast a devil?

49 Jesus answered, I have not a devil; but I honour my Father, and ye do dishonour me. 50 And I seek not mine own glory: there is one that seeketh and judgeth.

51 Verily, verily, I say unto you, If a man keep my saying, he shall never see death.

Jesus is referring to the eternal death from the judgment.

The religious leaders here are contending with the Word of God. Friends, I speak from personal experience. This is no different today. It is easier to remember what you have been told by others than to read the Word of God yourself. I want to commend you for reading what I consider a conservative commentary. Am I right on everything? No. There is only one perfect teacher and He was standing in front of these religious leaders. What were they doing? They were fighting with Him. If you read the Bible yourself, then the Word of God is in front of you also.

The Jews respond to Jesus. Verses 52-53:

52 Then said the Jews unto him, Now we know that thou [Jesus] hast a devil. Abraham is dead, and the prophets; and thou sayest, If a man keep my saying, he shall never taste of death.

53 Art thou greater than our father Abraham, which is dead? and the prophets are dead: whom makest thou thyself?

Jesus responds to their accusations. Everything that Jesus said was true. Verses 54-56:

54 Jesus answered, If I honour myself, my honour is nothing: it is my Father that honoureth me; of whom ye say, that he is your God:

55 Yet ye have not known him; but I know him: and if I should say, I know him not, I shall be a liar like unto you: but I know him, and keep his saying.

56 Your father Abraham rejoiced to see my day: and he saw it, and was glad.

This argument draws to its end. The Jews challenged His facts. Verse 57:

57 Then said the Jews unto him, Thou art not yet fifty years old, and hast thou seen Abraham?

In the next verse, there is something you should know about God's name. At the Burning Bush, God told Moses to go back to Egypt to free the people from bondage. Moses asked God whom should he say sent him, if they ask. Exodus 3:14:

14 And God said unto Moses, I AM THAT I AM: and he said, Thus shalt thou say unto the children of Israel, I AM hath sent me unto you.

With that information, read on. John 8:58:

58 Jesus said unto them, Verily, verily, I say unto you, <u>Before Abraham was, I am</u>.

Jesus, by these words, proclaims that He is God. Here is their response. Verse 59:

59 Then took they up stones to cast at him: but Jesus hid himself, and went out of the temple, going through the midst of them, and so passed by.

11

John 9

No longer in Jerusalem, Jesus continues His ministry by moving on. The following answers whether sin is the cause of disabilities. John 9:1-3:

1 And as Jesus passed by, he saw a man which was blind from his birth.

2 And his disciples asked him, saying, Master, who did sin, this man, or his parents, that he was born blind?

3 Jesus answered, Neither hath this man sinned, nor his parents: but that the works of God should be made manifest [made known] in him.

Many times, it is an opportunity for God's glory to be shown.

Jesus explains that He is only here for a short time. However, while He is in the world, He will do the work of the One Who sent Him. Verses 4-7:

> **4 I must work the works of him that sent me, while it is day: the night cometh, when no man can work. 5 As long as I am in the world, I am the light of the world.**
>
> **6 When he had thus spoken, he spat on the ground, and made clay of the spittle, and he anointed the eyes of the blind man with the clay,**
>
> **7 And said unto him, Go, wash in the pool of Siloam, (which is by interpretation, Sent.) He went his way therefore, and washed, and came seeing.**

I do not believe that anyone witnessed the healing. The locals, who knew this man, immediately noticed. Seeing he was healed, they wanted to know where Jesus was, but he did not know. Verses 8-12:

> **8 The neighbours therefore, and they which before had seen him that he was blind, said, Is not this he that sat and begged?**

9 Some said, This is he: others said, He is like him: but he said, I am he. 10 Therefore said they unto him, How were thine eyes opened?

11 He answered and said, A man that is called Jesus made clay, and anointed mine eyes, and said unto me, Go to the pool of Siloam, and wash: and I went and washed, and I received sight.

12 Then said they unto him, Where is he? He said, I know not.

This blind man who had been healed on the Sabbath was brought before the Pharisees for questioning. They sought to gain more evidence against Jesus. Verses 13-17:

13 They brought to the Pharisees him that aforetime was blind. 14 And it was the sabbath day when Jesus made the clay, and opened his eyes.

15 Then again the Pharisees also asked him how he had received his sight. He said unto them, He put clay upon mine eyes, and I washed, and do see.

16 Therefore said some of the Pharisees, This man is not of God, because he keepeth not the sabbath day. Others said, How can a man that is a sinner do such miracles? And there was a division among them.

17 They say unto the blind man again, What sayest thou of him, that he hath opened thine eyes? He said, He is a prophet.

The Pharisees did not believe the man, so they summoned his parents to refute his story. The parents feared these powerful men as you can see from their reaction. Verses 18-23:

18 But the Jews did not believe concerning him, that he had been blind, and received his sight, until they called the parents of him that had received his sight.

19 And they asked them, saying, Is this your son, who ye say was born blind? how then doth he now see? **20** His parents answered them and said, We know that this is our son, and that he was born blind:

21 But by what means he now seeth, we know not; or who hath opened his eyes, we know not: he is of age; ask him: he shall speak for himself.

22 These words spake his parents, because they feared the Jews: for the Jews had agreed already, that if any man did confess that he was Christ, he should be put out of the synagogue. 23 Therefore said his parents, He is of age; ask him.

The Pharisees concluded that he was healed and he should praise God. However, this man Jesus Who healed him was a sinner. Consider the man's reaction. Verses 24-34:

24 Then again called they the man that was blind, and said unto him, Give God the praise: we know that this man is a sinner.

25 He answered and said, Whether he be a sinner or no, I know not: one thing I know, that, whereas I was blind, now I see.

26 Then said they to him again, What did he to thee? how opened he thine eyes?

27 He answered them, I have told you already, and ye did not hear: wherefore would ye hear it again? will ye also be his disciples?

28 Then they reviled him, and said, Thou art his disciple; but we are Moses' disciples. 29 We know that God spake unto Moses: as for this fellow, we know not from whence [wherefrom] he is.

30 The man answered and said unto them, Why herein is a marvellous thing, that ye know not from whence he is, and yet he hath opened mine eyes.

31 Now we know that God heareth not sinners: but if any man be a worshipper of God, and doeth his will, him he heareth.

32 Since the world began was it not heard that any man opened the eyes of one that was born blind. 33 If this man were not of God, he could do nothing.

34 They answered and said unto him, Thou wast altogether born in sins, and dost thou teach us? And they cast him

out.

The Pharisees were not pleased that they should be questioned by a sinner. Who is he that he should teach them? Now, being done with him, they cast him out from their presence.

Later, Jesus met the man again and asked him a question every Jew should be asked. Verses 35-38:

> 35 **Jesus heard that they had cast him out; and when he had found him, he said unto him, Dost thou believe on the Son of God?**

> 36 **He answered and said, Who is he, Lord, that I might believe on him?**

> 37 **And Jesus said unto him, Thou hast both seen him, and it is he that talketh with thee.**

> 38 **And he said, Lord, I believe. And he worshipped him.**

Jesus makes a statement within the hearing of some Pharisees. Verses 39-41:

> 39 **And Jesus said, <u>For judgment I am</u>**

come into this world, that they which
see not might see; and that they which
see might be made blind.

40 **And some of the Pharisees which
were with him heard these words, and
said unto him, Are we blind also?**

41 **Jesus said unto them, If ye were blind,
ye should have no sin: but now ye say,
We see; therefore your sin remaineth.**

What does this mean? The man who was blind was
a sinner, but He saw the Messiah and believed. He
will be forgiven His sin. However, the Pharisees who
are sinners believe that they are righteous. Believing
themselves to see, they do not see the Son of God
Who stands before them. Therefore, they remain in
their sin for they choose not to see Him.

12

John 10

Take a moment and think about all the fakes and deceivers out in the world today. The Apostle Paul warns believers. It may seem odd to quote from the Apostle to the Gentiles, but this warning applies to all who seek after the knowledge of God. Colossians 2:8:

> 8 **Beware lest any man spoil you through philosophy and vain deceit, after the tradition of men, after the rudiments of the world, and not after Christ.**

Jesus' warns the children of Israel by comparing them to sheep. The sheep know their Shepherd and He knows His sheep. John 10:1-4:

> 1 **Verily, verily, I say unto you, He that entereth not by the door into the sheep-**

fold, but climbeth up some other way, the same is a thief and a robber.

2 But he that entereth in by the door is the shepherd of the sheep. 3 To him the porter openeth; and the sheep hear his voice: and he calleth his own sheep by name, and leadeth them out.

4 And when he putteth forth his own sheep, he goeth before them, and the sheep follow him: for they know his voice.

However, the sheep will not follow the voice of a stranger. Verse 5:

5 And a stranger will they not follow, but will flee from him: for they know not the voice of strangers.

Jesus used relatable stories to teach the people. In this agricultural society, many were farmers or raised livestock such as sheep. Verses 6-15:

6 This parable spake Jesus unto them: but they understood not what things they were which he spake unto them.

7 Then said Jesus unto them again, Verily, verily, I say unto you, I am the door of the sheep.

8 All that ever came before me are thieves and robbers: but the sheep did not hear them.

9 I am the door: by me if any man enter in, he shall be saved, and shall go in and out, and find pasture.

10 The thief cometh not, but for to steal, and to kill, and to destroy: I am come that they might have life, and that they might have it more abundantly.

11 I am the good shepherd: the good shepherd giveth his life for the sheep.

12 But he that is an hireling, and not the shepherd, whose own the sheep are not, seeth the wolf coming, and leaveth the sheep, and fleeth: and the wolf catcheth them, and scattereth the sheep.

13 The hireling fleeth, because he is an hireling, and careth not for the sheep.

14 <u>I am</u> the good shepherd, and know my sheep, and am known of mine.

15 As the Father knoweth me, even so know I the Father: and <u>I lay down my life for the sheep</u>.

Earlier, we discussed how the Kingdom of Israel was divided into the northern and southern kingdoms. The ten tribes of the north fell, were taken, and assimilated into a Gentile nation. They are sometimes referred to as "the lost children of Israel." This is not the case. God knows exactly where these sheep are. We see this in the following verses. Verse 16:

16 And other sheep I have, which are not of this fold: them also I must bring, and they shall hear my voice; and there shall be one fold, and one shepherd.

Jesus will restore the twelve tribes of Israel into one fold and He will be their Shepherd. Verses 17-18:

17 Therefore doth my Father love me, because I lay down my life, that I might take it again.

18 No man taketh it from me, but I lay it down of myself. I have power to lay it down, and I have power to take it again. This commandment have I received of my Father.

We see from the above that Jesus willingly lays down His life and that no man takes it from Him.

This caused a dispute among those who were listening to Jesus. Many believed that He was filled with a demon. Verses 19-21:

19 **There was a division therefore again among the Jews for these sayings.**

20 **And many of them said, He hath a devil, and is mad; why hear ye him?**

21 **Others said, These are not the words of him that hath a devil. Can a devil open the eyes of the blind?**

Jesus was in the Temple and He was surrounded by Jews demanding, "If thou be the Anointed One, tell us plainly." Verses 22-25:

22 **And it was at Jerusalem the feast of the dedication, and it was winter. 23 And Jesus walked in the temple in Solomon's porch.**

24 Then came the Jews round about him, and said unto him, How long dost thou make us to doubt? If thou be the Christ [Anointed One], tell us plainly.

25 Jesus answered them, I told you, and ye believed not: the works that I do in my Father's name, they bear witness of me.

He responds that He has already told them so, but they do not believe. He tells them that the miracles He has done "in my Father's name" are all the evidence that they need.

Jesus continues with the same parable concerning the sheep and their Shepherd. Verses 26-30:

26 But ye believe not, because ye are not of my sheep, as I said unto you. 27 <u>My sheep hear my voice, and I know them, and they follow me:</u>

28 <u>And I give unto them eternal life;</u> and they shall never perish, neither shall any man pluck them out of my hand.

29 My Father, which gave them [to] me, is greater than all; and no man is able to

pluck them out of my Father's hand. 30 I and my Father are one.

Verses 28-29 above are often used as proof texts that once someone is saved, their eternal salvation is secure. With the Gospel of the Kingdom, salvation for the believing Jew is secure unless, like their ancestors in the Wilderness, they lose faith. No one can take their salvation from them, but they can stop believing. To that end, Jesus said, "But he that shall endure unto the end, the same shall be saved" (Matt. 24:13). Kingdom Believers must continue to have faith and they must provide proof through their actions.

Their response confirms that the Jews rejected His claim in spite of the works He has done among them. Verses 31-39:

31 Then the Jews took up stones again to stone him.

32 Jesus answered them, Many good works have I shewed [shown] you from my Father; for which of those works do ye stone me?

33 The Jews answered him, saying, For a good work we stone thee not; but for blasphemy; and because that thou, be-

ing a man, makest thyself God.

34 Jesus answered them, Is it not written in your law, I said, Ye are gods? 35 If he called them gods, unto whom the word of God came, and the scripture cannot be broken;

36 Say ye of him, whom the Father hath sanctified, and sent into the world, Thou blasphemest; because I said, <u>I am the Son of God</u>?

37 If I do not the works of my Father, believe me not. 38 But if I do, though ye believe not me, believe the works: that ye may know, and believe, that the Father is in me, and I in him.

39 Therefore they sought again to take him: but he escaped out of their hand,

Jesus escaped from threatening situations before by simply walking away. He is the Son of God. Therefore, if Jesus is taken away to death, then it must be that His willing to be taken. Verses 40-42:

40 And went away again beyond Jordan into the place where John at first bap-

tized; and there he abode.

41 And many resorted [went] unto him, and said, John did no miracle: but all things that John spake of this man were true.

42 And many believed on him there.

13

John 11

Bethany is a village located just two miles from Jerusalem on the Mount of Olives. Here is the much loved story of Lazarus and his two sisters, Mary and Martha. John 11:1-4:

> 1 **Now a certain man was sick, named Lazarus, of Bethany, the town of Mary and her sister Martha. 2 (It was that Mary which anointed the Lord with ointment, and wiped his feet with her hair, whose brother Lazarus was sick.)**

> 3 **Therefore his sisters sent unto him, saying, Lord, behold, he whom thou lovest is sick. 4 When Jesus heard that, he said, This sickness is not unto death, but for the glory of God, that the Son of God might be glorified thereby.**

Do you remember the man who was blind since birth? His disciples asked Jesus, " Master, who did sin, this man, or his parents, that he was born blind?" (Jn. 9:2). Jesus replied, "Neither hath this man sinned, nor his parents: but that the works of God should be made manifest in him" (v. 3). Similarly, Jesus told Martha and Mary that Lazarus' sickness would not come to death, but rather bring glory to God.

These three were Jesus' friends and He loved them. In spite of the threat posed by the religious leaders, He would return. Verses 5-6:

> 5 **Now Jesus loved Martha, and her sister, and Lazarus. 6 When he had heard therefore that he was sick, he abode two days still in the same place where he was.**

Did you notice that Jesus tarried for two days? Verses 7-13:

> 7 **Then after that saith he to his disciples, Let us go into Judaea again.**
>
> 8 **His disciples say unto him, Master, the Jews of late sought to stone thee; and goest thou thither [there] again?**

9 Jesus answered, Are there not twelve hours in the day? If any man walk in the day, he stumbleth not, because he seeth the light of this world.

10 But if a man walk in the night, he stumbleth, because there is no light in him. 11 These things said he: and after that he saith unto them, Our friend Lazarus sleepeth; but I go, that I may awake him out of sleep.

12 Then said his disciples, Lord, if he sleep, he shall do well. 13 Howbeit Jesus spake of his death: but they thought that he had spoken of taking of rest in sleep.

Jesus referred to Lazarus as sleeping, but He meant dead. When the disciples misunderstood, He corrected them. Verses 14-15:

14 Then said Jesus unto them plainly, Lazarus is dead.

15 And I am glad for your sakes that I was not there, to the intent [purpose that] ye may believe; nevertheless let us go unto him.

Jesus' disciples were committed to Him. Concerned that the religious leaders may kill Him, they resolved to go as well to die with Him. Verses 16-17:

> 16 Then said Thomas, which is called Didymus, unto his fellow disciples, Let us also go, that we may die with him.

> 17 Then when Jesus came, he found that he [Lazarus] had lain in the grave four days already.

Due to its proximity to Jerusalem, many friends and family of the deceased were there. Do you remember that this tragedy should glorify God? We continue. Verses 18-22:

> 18 Now Bethany was nigh unto Jerusalem, about fifteen furlongs off: 19 And many of the Jews came to Martha and Mary, to comfort them concerning their brother.

> 20 Then Martha, as soon as she heard that Jesus was coming, went and met him: but Mary sat still in the house.

> 21 Then said Martha unto Jesus, Lord, if thou hadst been here, my brother had

not died. 22 But I know, that even now, whatsoever thou wilt ask of God, God will give it [to] thee.

Martha had remarkable faith in Jesus. She is confident in the resurrection of the dead, but Jesus speaks about Lazarus being restored to them now. Verses 23-27:

23 Jesus saith unto her, Thy brother shall rise again. 24 Martha saith unto him, <u>I know that he shall rise again in the resurrection at the last day</u>.

25 Jesus said unto her, <u>I am the resurrection, and the life: he that believeth in me, though he were dead, yet shall he live:</u> 26 <u>And whosoever liveth and believeth in me shall never die.</u> Believest thou this?

27 She saith unto him, Yea, Lord: <u>I believe that thou art the Christ, the Son of God</u>, which should come into the world.

We need to stop for a moment so that you do not miss this. That profession of faith is the same as the one Peter gave to Jesus. The Gospel of the Kingdom is different from the Gospel of Grace preached by the Apostle Paul. The Jews must profess faith in Jesus that He is their Messiah and the Son of God. That is the basis of salvation for the Jews. Due to their past, God requires that the Jews keep their faith until the end. When Jesus returns at the end, He will forgive their sins and grant them eternal life.

Martha is so excited the Jesus has arrived that she runs ahead to tell her sister Mary. Verses 28-34:

> 28 **And when she had so said, she went her way, and called Mary her sister secretly, saying, The Master is come, and calleth for thee. 29 As soon as she heard that, she arose quickly, and came unto him.**
>
> 30 **Now Jesus was not yet come into the town, but was in that place where Martha met him. 31 The Jews then which were with her in the house, and comforted her, when they saw Mary, that she rose up hastily and went out, followed her, saying, She goeth unto the grave to weep there.**
>
> 32 **Then when Mary was come where Jesus was, and saw him, she fell down at**

his feet, saying unto him, Lord, if thou hadst been here, my brother had not died.

33 When Jesus therefore saw her weeping, and the Jews also weeping which came with her, he groaned in the spirit, and was troubled,

34 And said, Where have ye laid him? They said unto him, Lord, come and see.

The following is said to be the shortest verse in the King James Bible, "Jesus wept." It shows that Jesus did not lack human emotion. Confident that Lazarus would be raised from the dead, He had empathy for his friends' sorrow. Verses 35-39:

35 Jesus wept. 36 Then said the Jews, Behold how he loved him! 37 And some of them said, Could not this man, which opened the eyes of the blind, have caused that even this man should not have died?

38 Jesus therefore again groaning in himself cometh to the grave. It was a cave, and a stone lay upon it.

39 Jesus said, Take ye away the stone. Martha, the sister of him that was dead, saith unto him, Lord, by this time he stinketh: for he hath been dead four days.

Enough time had passed and the decay of the body would have set in. The stench would be overwhelming. However, through their faith, the miraculous glory of God will be revealed. Verses 40-46:

40 Jesus saith unto her, Said I not unto thee, that, if thou wouldest believe, thou shouldest see the glory of God?

41 Then they took away the stone from the place where the dead was laid. And Jesus lifted up his eyes, and said, Father, I thank thee that thou hast heard me.

42 And I knew that thou hearest me always: but because of the people which stand by I said it, that they may believe that thou hast sent me.

43 And when he thus had spoken, he cried with a loud voice, Lazarus, come forth.

44 And he that was dead came forth, bound hand and foot with graveclothes: and his face was bound about with a napkin. Jesus saith unto them, Loose him, and let him go.

45 Then many of the Jews which came to Mary, and had seen the things which Jesus did, believed on him.

46 But some of them went their ways to the Pharisees, and told them what things Jesus had done.

We do not know why some went to inform the Pharisees. Since the purpose for raising Lazarus from the dead was to glorify God, I would like to believe they went to the Pharisees to proclaim that Jesus was the Son of God. Regardless of their reason, how did the Pharisees react? Verses 47-49:

47 Then gathered the chief priests and the Pharisees a council, and said, What do we? for this man doeth many miracles.

48 If we let him thus alone, all men will believe on him: and the Romans shall come and take away both our place and

nation. 49 And one of them, named Caiaphas, being the high priest that same year, said unto them, Ye know nothing at all,

There are certain statements in the Bible that I call proclamations. These are statements of truth spoken out loud to those to whom it is intended. In other words, "out of thine own mouth" do they judge themselves. Look at these statements being made by the Chief Priest of Israel. Verses 50-53:

50 Nor consider that it is expedient for us, that one man should die for the people, and that the whole nation perish not.

51 And this spake he not of himself: but being high priest that year, he prophesied that Jesus should die for that nation;

52 And not for that nation only, but that also he should gather together in one the children of God that were scattered abroad. 53 Then from that day forth they took counsel together for to put him to death.

It was not yet His time according to God's divine plan. So, Jesus went to Ephraim which is located in the hill-country of Judea and remained there. It is about thirteen miles northeast of Jerusalem. Verse 54:

> **54 Jesus therefore walked no more openly among the Jews; but went thence unto a country near to the wilderness, into a city called Ephraim, and there continued with his disciples.**

Passover is an important holiday with many preparations. As such, many from the countryside went into Jerusalem. There, the chief priests and Pharisees sought out Jesus that they may take Him. Verses 55-57:

> **55 And the Jews' passover was nigh [near] at hand: and many went out of the country up to Jerusalem before the passover, to purify themselves.**

> **56 Then sought they for Jesus, and spake among themselves, as they stood in the temple, What think ye, that he will not come to the feast?**

> **57 Now both the chief priests and the Pharisees had given a commandment,**

that, if any man knew where he were, he should shew [reveal] it, that they might take him.

14

John 12

With only a week before Passover, Lasarus was able to enjoy a meal with his sister and his Savior. Here, Mary does something unusual in the eyes of the disciples, but Jesus explains its purpose. John 12:1-3:

1 Then Jesus six days before the passover came to Bethany, where Lazarus was which had been dead, whom he raised from the dead.

2 There they made him a supper; and Martha served: but Lazarus was one of them that sat at the table with him.

3 Then took Mary a pound of ointment of spikenard, very costly, and anointed the feet of Jesus, and wiped his feet

with her hair: and the house was filled with the odour [fragrance] of the ointment.

Judas was the treasurer of the Twelve. He saw this as a tremendous waste of money that could be used elsewhere. Verses 4-8:

4 Then saith one of his disciples, Judas Iscariot, Simon's son, which should betray him,

5 Why was not this ointment sold for three hundred pence, and given to the poor? 6 This he said, not that he cared for the poor; but because he was a thief, and had the bag, and bare what was put therein.

7 Then said Jesus, Let her alone: against [for the preparation of] the day of my burying hath she kept this.

8 For the poor always ye have with you; but me ye have not always.

Mary anointed Jesus in preparation of His death and burial. The Gospel of Mark records Jesus as saying this. Mark 14:8-9:

8 She hath done what she could: she is come aforehand to anoint my body to the burying.

9 Verily I say unto you, Wheresoever this gospel shall be preached throughout the whole world, this also that she hath done shall be spoken of for a memorial of her.

Like today, news is more about sensationalism. People are not looking to learn something but to satisfy their curiosity. Such is the case here. John 12:9-11:

9 Much people of the Jews therefore knew that he was there: and they came not for Jesus' sake only, but that they might see Lazarus also, whom he had raised from the dead.

10 But the chief priests consulted that they might put Lazarus also to death; **11** Because that by reason of him many of the Jews went away, and believed on Jesus.

The crowds that came to Jerusalem for the feast looked for Jesus and Lazarus so they could point and stare at them. Verses 12-13:

> 12 On the next day much people that
> were come to the feast, when they heard
> that Jesus was coming to Jerusalem,

> 13 Took branches of palm trees, and
> went forth to meet him, and cried, Ho-
> sanna: <u>Blessed is the King of Israel that
> cometh in the name of the Lord.</u>

This fulfills the prophecy concerning Jesus' entrance
into Jerusalem as the King. Zechariah 9:9

> 9 Rejoice greatly, O daughter of Zion;
> shout, O daughter of Jerusalem: behold,
> thy King cometh unto thee: he is just,
> and having salvation; lowly, and riding
> upon an ass, and upon a colt the foal of
> an ass.

We continue with our text. John 12:14-18:

> 14 And Jesus, when he had found a
> young ass, sat thereon; as it is written,

> 15 Fear not, daughter of Sion [Zion]: be-
> hold, thy King cometh, sitting on an
> ass's colt.

16 These things understood not his disciples at the first: but when Jesus was glorified, then remembered they that these things were written of [about] him, and that they had done these things unto him.

17 The people therefore that was with him when he called Lazarus out of his grave, and raised him from the dead, bare [confirm the] record.

18 For this cause the people also met him, for that they heard that he had done this miracle.

As the people satisfied their curiosity, the Pharisees were concerned about everyone leaving them to follow after Him. They considered Jesus to be a charlatan. Verse 19:

19 The Pharisees therefore said among themselves, Perceive ye how ye prevail nothing? behold, the world is gone after him.

The following verse must be interpreted dispensationally. I have maintained throughout the gospels that Jesus came to fulfill the promises God made to their fathers. (See Romans 15:8.) The word "Greeks" below refers to "the Gentiles." If John had used the word "Grecian" it would have meant "Grecian Jews," but he used "Greeks." Therefore, it was certain Gentiles that came to see Jesus. Verses 20-22:

> 20 And there were certain Greeks among them that came up to worship at the feast:
>
> 21 The same came therefore to Philip, which was of Bethsaida of Galilee, and desired him, saying, Sir, we would see Jesus.
>
> 22 Philip cometh and telleth Andrew: and again Andrew and Philip tell Jesus.

Notice Jesus' response to His disciples. He did not speak with these Gentiles. Verses 23-24:

> 23 And Jesus answered them [Andrew and Philip], saying, The hour is come, that the Son of man should be glorified.
>
> 24 Verily, verily, I say unto you, Except a corn of wheat fall into the ground and die, it abideth alone: but if it die, it bringeth forth much fruit.

Jesus is the Messiah to Israel alone. Not until a seed falls to the ground and dies can "it bringeth forth much fruit" (v. 24).

Jesus changes the subject so as not to be questioned further. Salvation through the Kingdom Gospel is for the children of Abraham. Verses 25-26:

25 **He that loveth his life shall lose it; and he that hateth his life in this world shall keep it unto life eternal.**

26 **If any man serve me, let him follow me; and where <u>I am</u>, there shall also my servant be: if any man serve me, him will my Father honour.**

Jesus is both fully Man and fully God. See what the Apostle Paul wrote about Him. Colossians 1:15-17:

15 <u>**Who is the image of the invisible God**</u>**, the firstborn of every creature:**

16 <u>**For by him were all things created, that are in heaven, and that are in earth, visible and invisible, whether they be thrones, or dominions, or principalities, or powers: all things were created by him, and for him:**</u>

17 **And he is before all things, and by him all things consist.**

Let us consider His humanity. John 1:14:

14 **And the Word was made flesh, and dwelt among us, (and we beheld his glory, the glory as of the only begotten of the Father,) full of grace and truth.**

The above provides us with a better understanding of Jesus' human emotions. He was overwhelmed with the imminent crucifixion. John 12:27-28:

27 **Now is my soul troubled; and what shall I say? Father, save me from this hour: but for this cause [purpose] came I unto this hour.**

28 **Father, glorify thy name. Then came there a voice from heaven, saying, I have both glorified it, and will glorify it again.**

Jesus was not alone when God said this. Others overheard God and believed that it was thunder. Verse 29:

29 The people therefore, that stood by, and heard it, said that it thundered: others said, An angel spake to him.

He explains that this voice came for their benefit. The judgment of this world is coming. Those who believe on me will be saved. Verses 30-33:

30 Jesus answered and said, This voice came not because of me, but for your sakes.

31 Now is the judgment of this world: now shall the prince of this world be cast out.

32 And I, if I be lifted up from the earth, will draw all men unto me. 33 This he said, signifying what death he should die.

The Jews knew their Scripture. They ask Jesus about the prophecy concerning the Christ—the Anointed One. Verse 34:

34 The people answered him, We have heard out of the law that Christ abideth forever: and how sayest thou, The Son of man must be lifted up? who is this

Son of man?

Jesus refers to Himself as "the light." He tells them that the light will be with them for only a short time. The Light is the source of truth. Jesus came to earth to give Israel the light which is the guidance and knowledge they needed. They are to walk in that light while it is with them. Verses 35-36:

> 35 Then Jesus said unto them, Yet a little while is the light with you. Walk while ye have the light, lest darkness come upon you: for he that walketh in darkness knoweth not whither [where] he goeth.

> 36 While ye have light, believe in the light, that ye may be the children of light. These things spake Jesus, and departed, and did hide himself from them.

There was still a problem with the people believing. It was prophesied by Isaiah nearly seven hundred years ago Verses 37-41:

> 37 But though he had done so many miracles before them, yet they believed not on him:

38 That the saying of Esaias [Isaiah] the prophet might be fulfilled, which he spake, Lord, who hath believed our report? and to whom hath the arm of the Lord been revealed?

39 Therefore they could not believe, because that Esaias said again, 40 <u>He hath blinded their eyes, and hardened their heart; that they should not see with their eyes, nor understand with their heart, and be converted, and I should heal them.</u>

41 These things said Esaias, when he saw his [God's] glory, and spake of him.

Some of the religious leaders believed but said nothing because of fear of the others. Verses 42-43:

42 Nevertheless among the chief rulers also many believed on him; but because of the Pharisees they did not confess him, lest they should be put out of the synagogue:

43 For they loved the praise of men more than the praise of God.

Jesus speaks aloud as if making a declaration, It is all about the One Who sent Him. Verses 44-47:

> 44 **Jesus cried and said, <u>He that believeth on me, believeth not on me, but on him that sent me.</u> 45 And <u>he that seeth me seeth him that sent me.</u>**

> 46 **I am come [as] a light into the world, that whosoever believeth on me should not abide in darkness. 47 And <u>if any man hear my words, and believe not, I judge him not: for I came not to judge the world, but to save the world.</u>**

Judgment is being withheld until the end of the Tribulation which He calls "the last day." He warns them that they will be judged according to "the Word." In other words, they will be judged by Scripture, the Word of God. Verses 48-49:

> 48 **He that rejecteth me, and receiveth not my words, hath one that judgeth him: the word that I have spoken, the same shall judge him in the last day.**

> 49 **For I have not spoken of myself; but the Father which sent me, he gave me a commandment, what I should say, and**

what I should speak.

The above verse confirms that the office in which the Messiah was operating is that of Prophet. He spoke the words that the Father had given Him. At His Ascension into heaven, He sits at the right hand of the Father. (See Psalms 110:1.) He remains there until His return as King. We find that, until His return, Jesus holds the office of Priest Who intercedes for Israel. Hebrews 2:17:

> 17 **Wherefore in all things it behoved him [Jesus] to be made like unto his brethren, that <u>he might be a merciful and faithful high priest in things pertaining to God, to make reconciliation for the sins of the people</u> [Israel].**

As Prophet, the words that Jesus spoke were given to Him by the Father. John 12:50:

> 50 **And I know that his commandment is life everlasting: whatsoever <u>I speak therefore, even</u> [that is to say] <u>as the Father said unto me, so I speak.</u>**

15

John 13

The time of Jesus' earthly ministry was coming to a close. After the Passover, He and the Twelve were together. He wanted to prepare them for what was about to happen. John 13:1-5:

1 **Now before the feast of the passover, when Jesus knew that his hour was come that he should depart out of this world unto the Father, having loved his own which were in the world, he loved them unto the end.**

2 **And supper being ended, the devil having now put into the heart of Judas Iscariot, Simon's son, to betray him;**

3 **Jesus knowing that the Father had given all things into his hands, and that**

he was come from God, and went to God;

4 He riseth from supper, and laid aside his garments; and took a towel, and girded himself.

5 After that he poureth water into a bason, and began to wash the disciples' feet, and to wipe them with the towel wherewith he was girded.

Jesus came to Peter. He was a fisherman, plain and simple. He saw the world in black and white. Sometimes he was hesitant, but he was an all-in or nothing kind of guy. Jesus loved him all the same. Verses 6-10:

6 Then cometh he to Simon Peter: and Peter saith unto him, Lord, dost thou wash my feet?

7 Jesus answered and said unto him, What I do thou knowest not now; but thou shalt know hereafter.

8 Peter saith unto him, Thou shalt never wash my feet. Jesus answered him, If I wash thee not, thou hast no part with

me. 9 Simon Peter saith unto him, Lord, not my feet only, but also my hands and my head.

10 Jesus saith to him, He that is washed needeth not save [except] to wash his feet, but is clean every whit [bit]: and ye are clean, but not all [of you].

When Jesus said, "but not all [of you]," He was speaking about Judas who was with them. Verse 11:

11 For he knew who should betray him; therefore said he, Ye [you all] are not all clean.

This washing of the feet was done for a lesson. He wanted them to remember that the Lord came to serve and not be served. Verses 12-17:

12 So after he had washed their feet, and had taken his garments, and was set down again, he said unto them, Know ye what I have done to you?

13 Ye call me Master and Lord: and ye say well; for so I am. 14 If I then, your Lord and Master, have washed your feet; ye also ought to wash one another's

feet. 15 For I have given you an example, that ye should do as I have done to you.

16 Verily, verily, I say unto you, The servant is not greater than his lord; neither he that is sent greater than he that sent him. 17 If ye know these things, happy are ye if ye do them.

Jesus said that not all of them are clean. When Jesus chose Judas, He knew in advance what He would do. Yet, He chose him. God's plan will be fulfilled! Verse 18:

18 I speak not of you all: I know whom I have chosen: but that the scripture may be fulfilled, He that eateth bread with me hath lifted up his heel against me.

He informs His disciples of the betrayal and, following this, there will be certain events which must happen. None of these events are by accident. They have been foreordained by God in fulfillment of Scripture. Verses 19-20:

19 Now I tell you before it come, that, when it is come to pass, ye may believe that I am he.

20 Verily, verily, I say unto you, He that receiveth whomsoever I send receiveth me; and he that receiveth me receiveth him that sent me.

It must have been distressing for Jesus to be in the presence of the one who will betray Him. He tell the disciples. Verses 21-23:

21 When Jesus had thus said, he was troubled in spirit, and testified, and said, Verily, verily, I say unto you, that <u>one of you shall betray me</u>.

22 Then the disciples looked one on another, doubting of whom he spake. 23 Now there was leaning on Jesus' bosom one of his disciples, whom Jesus loved.

The youngest of the disciples was the Apostle John, the author of this gospel. It was getting late. While at the table, John rested his head on Jesus' chest as the meal had ended. Verses 24-30:

24 Simon Peter therefore beckoned to him [John], that he should ask who it should be of whom he spake. 25 He then lying on Jesus' breast saith unto him, Lord, who is it?

26 Jesus answered, He it is, to whom I shall give a sop, when I have dipped it. And when he had dipped the sop, he gave it to Judas Iscariot, the son of Simon.

27 And after the sop Satan entered into him. Then said Jesus unto him, That thou doest, do quickly. 28 Now no man at the table knew for what intent he spake this unto him.

29 For some of them thought, because Judas had the bag, that Jesus had said unto him, Buy those things that we have need of against the feast; or, that he should give something to the poor.

30 He [Judas] then having received the sop went immediately out: and it was night.

There is information about Judas' betrayal that is found in another gospel. Matthew 26:14-16:

14 Then one of the twelve, called Judas Iscariot, went unto the chief priests,

15 And said unto them, What will ye

give me, and I will deliver him unto you? And they covenanted with him for thirty pieces of silver.

16 And from that time he sought opportunity to betray him.

Throughout all the difficult challenges Jesus will face, He seeks to glorify His Father and see His mission through to the end. John 13:31-32:

31 Therefore, when he [Judas] was gone out, Jesus said, Now is the Son of man glorified, and God is glorified in him.

32 If God be glorified in him, God shall also glorify him in himself, and shall straightway glorify him.

There was very little time that they would be together. The same love He has for His disciples, He wants them to have for each other. Verses 33-35:

33 Little children, yet a little while I am with you. Ye shall seek me: and as I said unto the Jews, Whither [Where] I go, ye cannot come; so now I say to you.

34 A new commandment I give unto you,

<u>That ye love one another; as I have loved you, that ye also love one another.</u>

35 By this shall all men know that ye are my disciples, if ye have love one to another.

Peter is all-in. Nothing will stand in his way in His devotion to Jesus. At this point, Peter still has much to learn. Verses 36-38:

36 Simon Peter said unto him, Lord, whither goest thou? Jesus answered him, Whither [Where] I go, thou canst not follow me now; but thou shalt follow me afterwards.

37 Peter said unto him, Lord, why cannot I follow thee now? I will lay down my life for thy sake.

38 Jesus answered him, Wilt thou lay down thy life for my sake? Verily, verily, I say unto thee, The cock shall not crow, till thou hast denied me thrice.

16

John 14

What we call the Old Testament holds promises and prophecies that God made to Israel. One of the promises was that God would send them a Messiah. Looking at Jesus' earthly ministry, the Apostle Paul sums it up for the Gentiles. Romans 15:8:

> 8 Now I say that <u>Jesus Christ was a minister of the circumcision for the truth of God, to confirm the promises made unto the fathers:</u>

Some of the people accepted and believed Jesus, but most of the religious leaders rejected Him. For all who believe, they are not to worry. They must trust that God will provide for them. John 14:1-3:

> 1 Let not your heart be troubled: ye believe in God, believe also in me. 2 In my

> Father's house are many mansions: if it were not so, I would have told you. I go to prepare a place for you.
>
> 3 <u>And if I go and prepare a place for you, I will come again, and receive you unto myself; that where I am, there ye may be also.</u>

Please notice the order of the events listed above. (1) Jesus will go. (2) He will come again. Once He has returned, (3) He will receive His believers unto Himself. The Rapture is not for the believers of the Gospel of the Kingdom. It is for those who believe the Gospel of Grace preached by the Apostle Paul. For an in-depth explanation of both gospels, consider reading *Letters To Theophilus*.

Jesus is the Shepherd of Israel. His sheep know His voice. Wherever the Shepherd goes, His sheep will go with Him. In order to be saved, Israel must believe. They must have faith in Jesus, the Messiah and Son of God. Verses 4-7:

> 4 And whither [where] I go ye know, and the way ye know. 5 Thomas saith unto him, Lord, we know not whither [where] thou goest; and how can we know the way?

6 Jesus saith unto him, <u>I am the way, the truth, and the life: no man cometh unto the Father, but by me.</u>

7 If ye had known me, ye should have known my Father also: and from henceforth ye know him, and have seen him.

The point Jesus is making here is that He and the Father are one. If they have seen Jesus, then they have seen the Father.

Even His disciples struggle with understanding this. Verses 8-11:

8 Philip saith unto him, Lord, shew us the Father, and it sufficeth [is sufficient for] us.

9 Jesus saith unto him, Have I been so long time with you, and yet hast thou not known me, Philip? <u>he that hath seen me hath seen the Father;</u> and how sayest thou then, Shew us the Father?

10 Believest thou not that <u>I am in the Father, and the Father in me?</u> the words that I speak unto you I speak not of myself: but the Father that dwelleth in me, he doeth the works.

11 Believe me that I am in the Father, and the Father in me: or else believe me for the very works' sake.

They should believe His words and, if not, believe it because of the mighty miracles He performed.

Those who believe will do greater miracles once He is again with the Father. Verses 12-14:

12 Verily, verily, I say unto you, He that believeth on me, the works that I do shall he do also; and greater works than these shall he do; because I go unto my Father.

13 And whatsoever ye shall ask in my name, that will I do, that the Father may be glorified in the Son.

14 If ye shall ask any thing in my name, I will do it.

And, because of the believers' relationship with Jesus, He will answer their requests made in His name.

Jesus gives instructions to His believers concerning what they must do while they await His return. They must have faith (trust) and they must keep His commandments (obey). There is hymn written by John H. Sammis with these words: "Trust and obey, For there's no other way, To be happy in Jesus, But to trust and obey." Verses 15-18:

> 15 **If ye love me, keep my commandments. 16 And I will pray [ask] the Father, and he shall give you another Comforter, that he may abide with you for ever;**
>
> 17 **Even the Spirit of truth; whom the world cannot receive, because it seeth him not, neither knoweth him: but ye know him; for he dwelleth with you, and shall be in you.**
>
> 18 **I will not leave you comfortless: I will come to you.**

Although Jesus will soon be taken from them, He will send the Comforter Who will "comfort" or "console" them in His absence.

Jesus speaks of His imminent departure. Verses 19-20:

19 Yet a little while, and the world seeth me no more; but ye see me: because I live, ye shall live also.

20 At that day ye shall know that I am in my Father, and ye in me, and I in you.

He returns to His theme of trusting and obeying His message. Jesus reminds them of what they are expected to do. Verses 21-24:

21 He that hath my commandments, and keepeth them, he it is that loveth me: and he that loveth me shall be loved of my Father, and I will love him, and will manifest myself to him.

22 Judas saith unto him, not Iscariot, Lord, how is it that thou wilt manifest [make known] thyself unto us, and not unto the world?

23 Jesus answered and said unto him, If a man love me, he will keep my words: and my Father will love him, and we will come unto him, and make our abode with him.

24 He that loveth me not keepeth not my

sayings: and the word which ye hear is not mine, but the Father's [words] which sent me.

Jesus speaks about the Comforter Who is the Holy Spirit. The Comforter will be sent once He is in heaven. Jesus explains the purpose for the Comforter. Verses 25-27:

25 These things have I spoken unto you, being yet present with you.

26 But the Comforter, which is the Holy Ghost, whom the Father will send in my name, <u>he shall teach you all things, and bring all things to your remembrance, whatsoever I have said unto you.</u>

27 Peace I leave with you, my peace I give unto you: not as the world giveth, give I unto you. Let not your heart be troubled, neither let it be afraid.

John repeats the opening verse which is the central theme of this chapter: "Let not your heart be troubled" (v. 1). Their faith and obedience are the proof that they belong to God and, therefore, God will provide for them.

Speaking to those gathered, Jesus says his farewell and blesses each of them. Verses 28-29:

28 Ye have heard how I said unto you, I go away, and come again unto you. If ye loved me, ye would rejoice, because I said, I go unto the Father: for my Father is greater than I.

29 And now I have told you before it come to pass, that, when it is come to pass, ye might believe.

When all the Jesus has told them comes true, they are to remember and believe. Verse 30:

30 Hereafter I will not talk much with you: for the prince of this world cometh, and hath nothing in [to do with] me.

As the disciples and believers have been given commandments, so has God given Jesus commandments as well. Jesus is faithful to the Father to complete the will of the Father. Verse 31:

31 But that the world may know that I love the Father; and as the Father gave me commandment, even so I do. Arise, let us go hence [forth].

17

John 15

The culmination of His mission was approaching. Jesus continues to teach. John 15:1-3:

> 1 **I am the true vine, and my Father is the husbandman.**
>
> 2 <u>**Every branch in me that beareth not fruit he taketh away: and every branch that beareth fruit, he purgeth it, that it may bring forth more fruit.**</u>
>
> 3 **Now ye are clean through the word which I have spoken unto you.**

The believers of the Kingdom Gospel have been sanctified by the Word. Notice that they are required to produce fruit. If they fail to produce fruit, as evidence of their faith, they will be pruned from the true vine. Good works are the fruit that provide proof of a living faith. Jesus encourages them to continue to abide in Him. Verses 4-5:

> 4 **Abide in me, and I in you. As the branch cannot bear fruit of itself, except it abide in the vine; no more can ye, except ye abide in me.**

> 5 **I am the vine, ye are the branches: He that abideth in me, and I in him, the same bringeth forth much fruit: for without me ye can do nothing.**

Jesus uses this allegory. He is the vine and the believers are its branches. They receive their spiritual life from the vine. Those who remain in the vine will bear much fruit because of Him. Verses 6-8:

> 6 **If a man abide not in me, he is cast forth as a branch, and is withered; and men gather them, and cast them into the fire, and they are burned.**

> 7 **If ye abide in me, and my words abide in you, ye shall ask what ye will, and it shall be done unto you.**

> 8 <u>**Herein is my Father glorified, that ye**</u>

<u>bear much fruit</u>; so shall ye be my disciples.

Jesus is connected to the Father Who sent Him. Similarly, the believers, as the branches, are connected to Jesus Who is the vine. What holds this all together? The answer is love! Verses 9-12:

9 **As the Father hath loved me, so have I loved you:** <u>**continue ye in my love.**</u>

10 **If ye** <u>**keep my commandments,**</u> **ye shall abide in my love; even as I have kept my Father's commandments, and abide in his love.**

11 **These things have I spoken unto you, that my joy might remain in you, and that your joy might be full.**

12 <u>**This is my commandment, That ye love one another, as I have loved you.**</u>

We will pause for a moment and consider Abraham, the father of the children of Israel. It has to do with Abraham being called a "friend of God." Isaiah 41:8:

8 **But thou, Israel, art my servant, Jacob**

whom I have chosen, the seed of <u>Abraham my friend.</u>

God told Abraham to sacrifice his only son Isaac. Abraham believed God would still fulfill the covenant He had given him. He had faith in God so he trusted and obeyed. As he was about to slay his son, God stopped him. Therefore, dear reader, if you are "the seed of Abraham," then you must trust and obey God. If you do, then you will be like your father Abraham and receive the benefits.

We return to our text. John 15:13-15:

13 <u>Greater love hath no man than this, that a man lay down his life for his friends.</u> 14 <u>Ye are my friends, if ye do whatsoever I command you.</u>

15 Henceforth I call you not servants; for the servant knoweth not what his lord doeth: but <u>I have called you friends;</u> for all things that I have heard of [from] my Father I have made known unto you.

Jesus is treating the believing Jews not as servants, but as friends. He has shared with them what the Father has told Him. Verse 16:

16 Ye have not chosen me, but I have chosen you, and ordained you, that ye should go and bring forth fruit, and that your fruit should remain: that whatsoever ye shall ask of the Father in my name, he may give it you.

Believers are to love the other believers and expect that the world, who hated God's Son, will hate them also. Verses 17-20:

17 These things <u>I command you, that ye love one another</u>. 18 If the world hate you, ye know that it hated me before it hated you.

19 If ye were of the world, the world would love his own: but <u>because ye are not of the world, but I have chosen you out of the world, therefore the world hateth you</u>.

20 Remember the word that I said unto you, <u>The servant is not greater than his lord. If they have persecuted me, they will also persecute you</u>; if they have kept [regarded] my saying, they will keep [regard] yours also.

Those who heard or regarded the words spoken by Christ rejected, mocked, and killed Him. Like Him, the believers words will be rejected and they will be hated also.

Unbelieving Jews rejected Jesus. They did not believe in Him because they did not believe in the One Who sent Him. Those who do believe are to trust and obey the commandments of Jesus. He is the Vine and gets His life from the Father. The branches get their life from Jesus. Verses 21-24:

> **21 But all these things will they do unto you for my name's sake, because they know not him that sent me.**
>
> **22 If I had not come and spoken unto them, they had not had sin: but now they have no cloke for their sin.**
>
> **23 He that hateth me hateth my Father also.**
>
> **24 If I had not done among them the works which none other man did, they had not had sin: but now have they both seen and hated both me and my Father.**

God sent His Son Who came and did miracles

as He preached the good news—the Gospel of the Kingdom. God was with His people and walked among them. He taught them in person. Having seen Him in person, they hated Him. I believe that He is specifically referring to the religious leaders of Israel. Verse 25:

> 25 But this cometh to pass, that the word might be fulfilled that is written in their law, They hated me without a cause.

Soon, the believers will receive the Comforter Who is the Holy Spirit. He will remain with them and remind them of what the Son did and said while He was among them. And, He will inspire the eyewitnesses to write the Holy Bible. Verses 26-27:

> 26 But when the Comforter is come, whom I will send unto you from the Father, even [that is to say] the Spirit of truth, which proceedeth from the Father, he shall testify of me:

> 27 And ye also shall bear witness, because ye have been with me from the beginning.

18

John 16

We must not forget that the four gospels were written "to" the Jews. Gentiles can read them to learn what God has planned for His people. The gospels are a continuation of the Old Testament and do not apply to the Gentiles. In the following, Jesus warns the Kingdom Believers that they will be persecuted. His intent is not to frighten them, but to prepare them for what will happen. John 16:1-4:

1 These things have I spoken unto you, that ye should not be offended.

2 They shall put you out of the synagogues: yea, the time cometh, that whosoever killeth you will think that he doeth God service.

3 And these things will they do unto

you, because they have not known the Father, nor me.

4 But these things have I told you, that when the time shall come, ye may remember that I told you of them. And these things I said not unto you at the beginning, because I was with you.

As Jesus shares what will happen, the believers are filled with sorrow. They are losing their Messiah and will not see Him again. It is for that reason that Jesus will send them the Comforter Who will abide with them. Verses 5-11:

5 But now I go my way to him that sent me; and none of you asketh me, Whither [Where] goest thou? 6 But because I have said these things unto you, sorrow hath filled your heart.

7 Nevertheless I tell you the truth; It is expedient [beneficial] for you that I go away: for if I go not away, the Comforter will not come unto you; but if I depart, I will send him unto you.

8 And when he is come, he will reprove the world of [1] sin, and of [2] righteous-

ness, and of [3] judgment:

9 **Of [1] sin, because they believe not on me;**

10 **Of [2] righteousness, because I go to my Father, and ye see me no more;**

11 **Of [3] judgment, because the prince of this world is judged.**

The title "prince of this world" refers to Satan who holds sway over the world by sin. Those who sin are in bondage. It is for that reason that Jesus came to set the captives free.

Let us pause for a moment. Here is an interesting story. Jesus was led out into the Wilderness to be tested following His baptism. Upon returning, He began His ministry in His home town synagogue. He was called to the bema to read from the Scripture. When He had finished reading, He returned to His seat, and all eyes were upon Him. The Jews knew their Scripture and Jesus stopped in mid-verse just before the word "and." He makes a proclamation. He said, "This day is this scripture fulfilled in your ears" (Lk. 4:21). What was He talking about and why did He stop mid-verse?

Jesus was reading from the prophet Isaiah as he spoke before the synagogue. These were devout Jews and many knew Him as a child. Luke 4:17-20:

> 17 **And there was delivered unto him the book of the prophet Esaias. And when he had opened the book, he found the place where it was written,**
>
> 18 **The Spirit of the Lord is upon me, because he hath anointed me to preach the gospel to the poor; he hath sent me to heal the brokenhearted, to preach deliverance to the captives, and recovering of sight to the blind, to set at liberty them that are bruised,** 19 **To preach the acceptable year of the Lord.**
>
> 20 **And he closed the book, and he gave it again to the minister, and sat down.**

Jesus read from Isaiah, but He stopped midway in the last verse. Those is attendance knew this and, then, He make a public proclamation. Isaiah 61:1-2a:

> 1 **The Spirit of the Lord GOD is upon me; because the LORD hath anointed me to preach good tidings unto the**

meek; he hath sent me to bind up the brokenhearted, to proclaim liberty to the captives, and the opening of the prison to them that are bound;

2a To proclaim the acceptable year of the LORD . . .

Let us look at the remainder of the verse. Verse 2b:

2b . . . and the day of vengeance of our God; to comfort all that mourn;

Here is the reason that Jesus stopped mid-verse. The latter portion of the verse applies to the future. It applies to the seven years of the coming testing of Israel. Let us confirm this. Jeremiah 30:4-9:

4 And these are the words that the LORD spake concerning Israel and concerning Judah. 5 For thus saith the LORD; We have heard a voice of trembling, of fear, and not of peace.

6 Ask ye now, and see whether a man doth travail with child? wherefore do I see every man with his hands on his loins, as a woman in travail, and all faces are turned into paleness?

7 Alas! for <u>that day is great</u>, so that none is like it: it is even <u>the time of Jacob's trouble; but he shall be saved out of it.</u>

8 For it shall come to pass in that day, saith the LORD of hosts, that I will break his yoke from off thy neck, and will burst thy bonds, and strangers shall no more serve themselves of him:

9 <u>But they shall serve the LORD their God, and David their king, whom I will raise up unto them.</u>

For further details and explanations, consider reading *The Glorious Destiny of Israel: The Fulfillment of God's Promises and Prophecies to Israel.*

We continue with our text. John 16:12-14:

12 I have yet many things to say unto you, but ye cannot bear them now.

13 Howbeit when he, the Spirit of truth, is come, he will guide you into all truth: for he shall not speak of himself; but whatsoever he shall hear, that shall he speak: and he will shew you things to come.

14 He shall glorify me: for he shall receive of mine [from me], and shall shew
it unto you.

God is working towards the complete restoration of His Creation. In the end, it is God's will to
hand over to Jesus all things. How long with the risen
Jesus be seated beside God the Father? Notice for
how long. Psalms 110:1:

1 The LORD said unto my Lord, Sit thou
at my right hand, <u>until I make thine enemies thy footstool</u>.

Now, with this information, look at John16:15:

15 All things that the Father hath are
mine: therefore said I, that he shall take
of mine, and shall shew it unto you.

Jesus speaks about His departure, the Ascension,
and His return, the Second Coming. In the meantime,
He is seated at the Father's right hand. Verses 16-18:

16 A little while, and ye shall not see me:
and again, a little while, and ye shall see
me, because I go to the Father.

17 Then said some of his disciples

among themselves, What is this that he saith unto us, A little while, and ye shall not see me: and again, a little while, and ye shall see me: and, Because I go to the Father?

18 They said therefore, What is this that he saith, A little while? we cannot tell what he saith.

Jesus knew that His disciples did not understand, so He responded. Verses 19-20:

19 Now Jesus knew that they were desirous to ask him, and said unto them, Do ye enquire among yourselves of that I said, A little while, and ye shall not see me: and again, a little while, and ye shall see me?

20 Verily, verily, I say unto you, That ye shall weep and lament, but the world shall rejoice: and <u>ye shall be sorrowful, but your sorrow shall be turned into joy</u>.

He compares this to a mother in labor. At first, there is pain, anguish, and much sorrow. However, there is joy when the child is presented to her. Verses

21-22:

> 21 A woman when she is in travail hath sorrow, because her hour is come: but as soon as she is delivered of the child, she remembereth no more the anguish, for joy that a man is born into the world.

> 22 And ye now therefore have sorrow: but I will see you again, and your heart shall rejoice, and your joy no man taketh from you.

The words "that day" have a particular meaning. There will be great turmoil during the seven years. Daniel's prophecy has seven remaining years after the crucifixion until the Kingdom is established. During this perilous seven years, they must ask God, because they cannot ask Jesus until He is the Victorious King. Verses 23-26:

> 23 And in that day ye shall ask me nothing. Verily, verily, I say unto you, Whatsoever ye shall ask the Father in my name, he will give it you.

> 24 Hitherto have ye asked nothing in my name: ask, and ye shall receive, that your joy may be full.

25 These things have I spoken unto you in proverbs: but the time cometh, when I shall no more speak unto you in proverbs, but I shall shew you plainly of the Father.

26 At that day ye shall ask in my name: and I say not unto you, that I will pray [ask] the Father for you:

The Father will answer the believers' requests because they have loved His Son. Verses 27-28:

27 For the Father himself loveth you, because ye have loved me, and have believed that I came out from God.

28 I came forth from the Father, and am come into the world: again, I leave the world, and go to the Father.

The disciples were common men, mostly fisherman, who were laborers and not highly educated men. They asked Jesus to simplify this for them. Verses 29-30:

29 His disciples said unto him, Lo, now speakest thou plainly, and speakest no proverb.

30 Now are we sure that thou knowest all things, and needest not that any man should ask thee: by this we believe that thou camest forth from God.

Jesus responds by asking them if they believe Who He said that He is. Verse 31:

31 Jesus answered them, Do ye now believe?

In the Gospel of Matthew, He tells them that the sheep will soon be scattered once He is taken from them. Matthew 26:31:

31 Then saith Jesus unto them, All ye shall be offended because of me this night: for it is written, <u>I will smite the shepherd, and the sheep of the flock shall be scattered abroad.</u>

The above verse is similar to what we find in our current text. John 16:32-33:

32 Behold, the hour cometh, yea, is now come, that <u>ye shall be scattered</u>, every man to his own, and shall leave me alone: and yet I am not alone, because the Father is with me.

33 These things I have spoken unto you, that in me ye might have peace. In the world ye shall have tribulation: but be of good cheer; I have overcome the world.

It will not be long before the Shepherd will be taken from them. All that Jesus has spoken will come back to them. Although they did not fulling understand Jesus' words, at the appropriate time, they will understand.

19

John 17

God's objective is the restoration of Creation. He will achieve this through His Son. Jesus will remain faithful and execute the will of His Father. Look below. We see that Jesus has faith and trusts His Father. Trust is the proof of faith! We see that Jesus is committed to obeying His Father's will. Let us notice to Whom Jesus turns when the going gets tough? He depends on God to complete His mission. John 17:1-4:

> 1 **These words spake Jesus, and lifted up his eyes to heaven, and said, <u>Father, the hour is come; glorify thy Son, that thy Son also may glorify thee:</u>**
>
> 2 **As thou hast given him power over all flesh, that he should give eternal life to as many as thou hast given him.**

3 And this is life eternal, that they might know thee the only true God, and Jesus Christ, whom thou hast sent.

4 I have glorified thee on the earth: <u>I have finished the work which thou gavest me to do</u>.

With His work on earth completed, He looks towards the final task where He may say, "It is finished" (Jn. 19:30). Now, He calls upon the Father to complete this work in Him. Verse 5:

5 And now, <u>O Father, glorify thou me with thine own self with the glory which I had with thee before the world was</u>.

The above verse is an excellent proof text to support that Jesus and the Father shared the glory before Creation. Verses 6-7:

6 I have manifested [made known] thy name unto the men which thou gavest me out of the world: thine they were, and thou gavest them [to] me; and they have kept thy word.

7 Now they have known that all things

whatsoever thou hast given me are of [from] thee.

Jesus came and spoke not His own words, but the words given to Him by the Father. When Jesus dies, it will be the Father Who resurrects Him from the dead. That is the trust that Jesus has in the Father. Verse 8:

> 8 For I have given unto them the words which thou gavest me; and they have received them, and have known surely that I came out from thee, and they have believed that thou didst send me.

Jesus prays for the disciples who believe on Him. They believe that He is the Messiah and the Son of God. Verses 9-12:

> 9 I pray for them: I pray not for the world, but for them which thou hast given me; for they are thine.

> 10 And all mine are thine, and thine are mine; and I am glorified in them.

> 11 And now I am no more in the world, but these are in the world, and I come to thee. Holy Father, keep through thine

own name those whom thou hast given me, that they may be one, as we are.

12 While I was with them in the world, I kept them in thy name: those that thou gavest me I have kept, and none of them is lost, but [except] the son of perdition; that the scripture might be fulfilled.

All of the disciples He kept except for Judas who betrayed Him. Judas is "the son of perdition" because "perdition" means "utter ruin or damnation."

Interceding on behalf of the disciples, Jesus prays for joy, protection from the world, and protection from evil. Verses 13-15:

13 And now come I to thee; and these things I speak in the world, that they might have my joy fulfilled in themselves.

14 I have given them thy word; and the world hath hated them, because they are not of the world, even [that is to say] as I am not of the world.

15 I pray not that thou shouldest take them out of the world, but that thou

shouldest keep them from the evil.

Below, the word "sanctify" means "to separate from the world" and be dedicated to God. Jesus asks that His disciples remain separate and unaffected by the world. Verses 16-17:

> 16 **They are not of the world, even as I am not of the world.** 17 <u>**Sanctify them through thy truth: thy word is truth.**</u>

How can Kingdom Believers be sanctified? We find the answer above. Believers are sanctified and separated from the world through the Word of Truth. The Word of Truth is the Bible!

In the verses below, Jesus says that He sanctifies Himself that they might be sanctified. Jesus is perfect. He has no need to be made "more holy." Remember, sanctify means being made separate unto God just as Jesus separated Himself from the world. Verses 18-19:

> 18 **As thou hast sent me into the world, even so have I also sent them into the world.**
>
> 19 **And for their sakes I sanctify myself, that they also might be sanctified**

through the truth.

Jesus prays not only for His disciples, but also those who will believe their testimony. This includes those who read their written testimony, the Holy Bible, and believe. Verse 20:

> 20 **Neither pray I for these alone, but for them also which shall believe on me through their word;**

Jesus asks His Father for unity among the believers. He wants these believers to share what the Father and Son share. Verses 21-23:

> 21 **That they all may be one; as thou, Father, art in me, and I in thee, that they also may be one in us: that the world may believe that thou hast sent me.**

> 22 **And the glory which thou gavest me I have given them; that they may be one, even as we are one:**

> 23 **I in them, and thou in me, that they may be made perfect in one; and that the world may know that thou hast sent me, and hast loved them, as thou hast loved me.**

Finally, Jesus addresses the future and His return. He wants these believers to be with Him and see the glory of the coming Kingdom. Verses 24-26:

24 **Father, I will that they also, whom thou hast given me, be with me where I am; that they may behold my glory, which thou hast given me: for thou lovedst me before the foundation of the world.**

25 **O righteous Father, the world hath not known thee: but I have known thee, and these have known that thou hast sent me.**

26 **And I have declared unto them thy name, and will declare it: that the love wherewith thou hast loved me may be in them, and I in them.**

John ends with making it clear that the love the Father and Son share, should be in the believers also.

20

John 18

The Apostle John chose not to include details about the Passover meal and Jesus' dialogue with His disciples. You can read them in the three other gospels: Matthew 26:20-31, Mark 14:16-27, and Luke 22:14-46. Instead, John begins this chapter after the Passover meal was finished. John 18:1-3:

1 **When Jesus had spoken these words, he went forth with his disciples over the brook Cedron, where was a garden, into the which he entered, and his disciples.**

2 **And Judas also, which betrayed him, knew the place: for Jesus ofttimes resorted thither with his disciples.**

3 **Judas then, having received a band of men and officers from the chief priests**

and Pharisees, cometh thither with lanterns and torches and weapons.

Once Judas and the band of armed men had arrived to apprehend Him, they confirm the One whom they sought. Verses 4-6:

> 4 Jesus therefore, knowing all things that should come upon him, went forth, and said unto them, Whom seek ye?
>
> 5 They answered him, Jesus of Nazareth. Jesus saith unto them, <u>I am he</u>. And Judas also, which betrayed him, stood with them. 6 <u>As soon then as he had said unto them, I am he, they went backward, and fell to the ground.</u>

Before Moses left for Egypt, he asked God for His name. This was in case the children of Israel should ask him Who had sent him. Here is God's response. Exodus 3:14:

> 14 And God said unto Moses, I AM THAT I AM: and he said, Thus shalt thou say unto the children of Israel, I AM hath sent me unto you.

It was for this reason that the crowd of men all fell

backwards. For those who bowl, that is called a strike where all the pins fall down.

This caused confusion, so Jesus started again. John 18:7-8:

> 7 **Then asked he them again, Whom seek ye? And they said, Jesus of Nazareth.**

> 8 **Jesus answered, I have told you that I am he: if therefore ye seek me, let these [others] go their way:**

All of the gospels include a reference to the striking of the Shepherd and His sheep scattering. He asked that the other with Him be let go. Verse 9:

> 9 **That the saying might be fulfilled, which he spake, Of them which thou gavest me have I lost none.**

There is a curious verse in Luke just before they left the Passover meal. The disciples respond to Jesus' comment about a sword. Luke 22:38-39:

> 38 **And they said, Lord, behold, here are two swords. And he said unto them, It is enough.**

39 And he came out, and went, as he was wont [custom], to the mount of Olives; and his disciples also followed him

I believe that the following incident prevented the mob from killing Jesus as it struck the group with fear. The injury caused by Peter's sword is immediately healed by Jesus. (See Luke 22:50-51.) John 18:10-11:

> **10** Then Simon Peter having a sword drew it, and smote the high priest's servant, and cut off his right ear. The servant's name was Malchus.

> **11** Then said Jesus unto Peter, Put up thy sword into the sheath: the cup which my Father hath given me, shall I not drink it?

After Jesus was arrested, they "brought him into the high priest's house" (Lk. 22:54). Notice the words of the high priest. Verses 12-14:

> **12** Then the band and the captain and officers of the Jews took Jesus, and bound him,

> **13** And led him away to Annas first; for

he was father in law to Caiaphas, which was the high priest that same year.

14 Now Caiaphas was he, which gave counsel to the Jews, that <u>it was expedient that one man should die for the people</u>.

Peter and another disciple followed. Verses 15-18:

15 And Simon Peter followed Jesus, and so did another disciple: that disciple was known unto the high priest, and went in with Jesus into the palace of the high priest.

16 But Peter stood at the door without [outside]. Then went out that other disciple, which was known unto the high priest, and spake unto her that kept the door, and brought in Peter.

17 Then saith the damsel that kept the door unto Peter, Art not thou also one of this man's disciples? He saith, I am not.

18 And the servants and officers stood there, who had made a fire of coals; for it was cold: and they warmed them-

selves: and Peter stood with them, and warmed himself.

They interrogated Jesus like a criminal and asked Him questions. Verses 19-21:

19 The high priest then asked Jesus of [about] his disciples, and of his doctrine.

20 Jesus answered him, I spake openly to the world; I ever [continually] taught in the synagogue, and in the temple, whither [where] the Jews always resort; and in secret have I said nothing.

21 Why askest thou me? ask them which heard me, what I have said unto them: behold, they know what I said.

Jesus' honest and direct response results in an open handed slap. It was a truthful answer, but they thought He was being insulant. Verses 22-24:

22 And when he had thus spoken, one of the officers which stood by struck Jesus with the palm of his hand, saying, Answerest thou the high priest so?

23 Jesus answered him, If I have spoken evil, bear [provide a] witness of the evil: but if well [true], why smitest thou me?

24 Now Annas had sent him bound unto Caiaphas the high priest.

Annas was a former high priest and father-in-law to Caiaphas, the present chief priest. Jesus was now sent on to him. Meanwhile, Peter waited outside. In the cool of the early morning, he stood beside a fire warming himself with others. Verses 25-27:

25 And Simon Peter stood and warmed himself. They said therefore unto him, Art not thou also one of his disciples? He denied it, and said, I am not.

26 One of the servants of the high priest, being his kinsman whose ear Peter cut off, saith, Did not I see thee in the garden with him? **27** Peter then denied again: and immediately the cock crew.

Jesus told Peter that he would deny Him three times before the cock crowed. It happened just as Jesus said that it would.

Jesus was then taken to the judgment hall of

the civil magistrate, Pontius Pilate. He served the Emperor Tiberius as governor over the Roman province of Judaea. Verses 28-29

> 28 Then led they Jesus from Caiaphas unto the hall of judgment: and it was early; and they themselves went not into the judgment hall, lest they should be defiled; but that they might eat the passover.

> 29 Pilate then went out unto them, and said, What accusation bring ye against this man?

The religious leaders of Israel do not answer Pilate's question. They simply state what appears to be true by their bringing Jesus to him. Verse 30:

> 30 They answered and said unto him, If he were not a malefactor, we would not have delivered him up unto thee.

Pilate does not want to assume the responsibility of judging a man according to their religious customs. But, as they state, only Pilate has the authority to put a man to death. It is for that reason that they brought Jesus to him. Verses 31-32:

31 Then said Pilate unto them, Take ye him, and judge him according to your law. The Jews therefore said unto him, <u>It is not lawful for us to put any man to death</u>:

32 That the saying of Jesus might be fulfilled, which he spake, signifying what death he should die.

Pilate asks the accused directly, "Art thou the King of the Jews?" Jesus does not answer but instead asks him if that statement is his own or the others who accuse him. Verses 33-34:

33 Then Pilate entered into the judgment hall again, and called Jesus, and said unto him, Art thou the King of the Jews?

34 Jesus answered him, Sayest thou this thing of thyself, or did others tell it thee of me?

Let us pause for a moment. Jesus is brought by the leaders of Israel to the civil magistrate because only he has the legal power to execute someone. They present their charges to Pilate which are that Jesus claims to be the King of the Jews. When Pilate asks Jesus about this, He inquires if this is his own belief or did someone else tell him this. Pilate confirms that it is His own nation and chief priests who charge Him. Verses 35-36:

> **35 Pilate answered, Am I a Jew? Thine own nation and the chief priests have delivered thee unto me: what hast thou done?**

> **36 Jesus answered, <u>My kingdom is not of this world: if my kingdom were of this world, then would my servants fight, that I should not be delivered to the Jews</u>: but now is my kingdom not from hence [here].**

Pilate asks Him if He is a king. Verse 37:

> **37 Pilate therefore said unto him, Art thou a king then? Jesus answered, Thou sayest that I am a king. To this end was I born, and for this cause came I into the world, that I should bear witness unto the truth. Every one that is of the truth heareth my voice.**

Hearing Jesus refer to "the truth," Pilate ends his interview by asking a question that non-believers still ask today, "What is truth?" There is a lot of relative truth. Each person has their own "relative" truth, but there is only one "absolute" truth. Absolute truth proceeds from the mouth of God. It is pure, unchanging, and lasts for eternity. Verse 38:

> 38 Pilate saith unto him, What is truth? And when he had said this, he went out again unto the Jews, and saith unto them, I find in him no fault at all.

In order to placate the Jews during Passover, Pilate suggests a means by which they can accomplish their desired outcome.

The Gospel of Matthew provides more details of the event. Matthew 27:15-26

> 15 Now at that feast the governor was wont [custom] to release unto the people a prisoner, whom they would [wished]. 16 And they had then a notable prisoner, called Barabbas.

> 17 Therefore when they were gathered together, Pilate said unto them, Whom will ye that I release unto you? Barabbas, or Jesus which is called Christ?

18 For he knew that for envy they [the Jews] had delivered him.

19 When he was set down on the judgment seat, his wife sent unto him, saying, Have thou nothing to do with that just man: for I have suffered many things this day in a dream because of him.

20 But the chief priests and elders persuaded the multitude that they should ask [for] Barabbas, and destroy Jesus.

21 The governor answered and said unto them, Whether of the twain [two] will ye that I release unto you? They said, Barabbas.

22 Pilate saith unto them, What shall I do then with Jesus which is called Christ? They all say unto him, Let him be crucified.

23 And the governor said, Why, what evil hath he done? But they cried out the more, saying, Let him be crucified.

24 When Pilate saw that he could prevail

nothing, but that rather a tumult was made, he took water, and washed his hands before the multitude, saying, I am innocent of the blood of this just person: see ye to it.

25 <u>Then answered all the people, and said, His blood be on us, and on our children.</u>

26 Then released he Barabbas unto them: and when he had scourged Jesus, he delivered him to be crucified.

With that, we return to the Apostle John's account. John 18:39-40:

39 But ye have a custom, that I should release unto you one at the passover: will [desire] ye therefore that I release unto you the King of the Jews?

40 <u>Then cried they all again, saying, Not this man, but Barabbas.</u> Now Barabbas was a robber.

At the urging of the chief priests and Pharisees, the people chose Barabbas, a robber. Israel chose to crucify the Son of God based upon the charge that Jesus claimed to be "the King of the Jews." Thus, Isaiah's prophesy was fulfilled. Isaiah 53:6-7 :

> 6 **All we like sheep have gone astray; we have turned every one to his own way; and <u>the LORD hath laid on him the iniquity of us all</u>.**

> 7 **He was oppressed, and he was afflicted, yet he opened not his mouth: <u>he is brought as a lamb to the slaughter</u>, and as a sheep before her shearers is dumb, so he openeth not his mouth.**

Jesus was the Lamb of God. On this Passover feast, He would become Israel's Passover Lamb.

21

John 19

Think for a moment about a computer program. Once the program is initiated, assuming there is no error, it will continue until it is completed. It is like the sovereign will of God. Prophecies written hundreds of years beforehand are, like computer programs, running in the background. In the gospel records, we can see God's program running. His restoration of Creation centers around Jesus. Eyewitnesses have recorded it! John 19:1-3:

1 **Then Pilate therefore took Jesus, and scourged him. 2 And the soldiers platted [weaved] a crown of thorns, and put it on his head, and they put on him a purple robe,**

3 **And said, Hail, King of the Jews! and they smote him with their hands.**

Prophecy, when completed, becomes a testimony to the faithfulness of God. Consider the prophet who testified to the children of Israel over seven hundred years before it happened. Isaiah 53:3-5:

> 3 <u>He is despised and rejected of [by] men</u>; a man of sorrows, and acquainted with grief: and <u>we hid as it were our faces from him</u>; <u>he was despised, and we esteemed him not.</u>
>
> 4 Surely <u>he hath borne our griefs</u>, and <u>carried our sorrows</u>: yet <u>we did esteem him stricken, smitten of God, and afflicted.</u>
>
> 5 But <u>he was wounded for our transgressions</u>, <u>he was bruised for our iniquities</u>: the chastisement [punishment] of our peace was upon him; and <u>with his stripes we are healed.</u>

Pilate appears before the crowds again to show them the King of the Jews. Verses 19:4-5:

> 4 Pilate therefore went forth again, and saith unto them, Behold, I bring him forth to you, that ye may know that I find no fault in him.

5 Then came Jesus forth, wearing the crown of thorns, and the purple robe. And Pilate saith unto them, <u>Behold the man!</u>

Consider the implications of their response for the children of Israel. Verses 6-7:

6 When the chief priests therefore and officers saw him, they cried out, saying, Crucify him, crucify him. Pilate saith unto them, Take ye him, and crucify him: for I find no fault in him.

7 The Jews answered him, We have a law, and by our law he ought to die, because he made himself the Son of God.

Pilate's wife warned him about a dream she had concerning this Man. He was aware that Jesus was innocent of their charges. It was their pride that brought Jesus before him. Therefore, he returned to speak with Jesus again. Verses 8-11:

8 When Pilate therefore heard that saying, he was the more afraid; **9** And went again into the judgment hall, and saith unto Jesus, Whence [Wherefrom] art thou? But Jesus gave him no answer.

10 Then saith Pilate unto him, Speakest thou not unto me? knowest thou not that I have power to crucify thee, and have power to release thee?

11 Jesus answered, Thou couldest have no power at all against me, except it were given thee from above: therefore he that delivered me unto thee hath the greater sin.

Pilate wanted to release Jesus, but the religious Jews persisted even threatening that he advocated for Someone Who spoke against Caesar. Verses 12-13:

12 And from thenceforth Pilate sought to release him: but the Jews cried out, saying, If thou let this man go, thou art not Caesar's friend: whosoever maketh himself a king speaketh against Caesar.

13 When Pilate therefore heard that saying, he brought Jesus forth, and sat down in the judgment seat in a place that is called the Pavement, but in the Hebrew, Gabbatha.

For the Jews, the time of day is measured beginning at 6 A.M. So, the sixth hour of the day would be noontime. Time is short for the Passover will begin about 6 P.M. and preparations must be made. Pilate brought Jesus before the crowd of Jews gathered. Notice that God has him use the words, "Behold your King!" Remember their response. Verses 14-15:

14 **And it was the preparation of the passover, and about the sixth hour: and he saith unto the Jews, <u>Behold your King!</u>**

15 **But they cried out, <u>Away with him, away with him, crucify him</u>. Pilate saith unto them, <u>Shall I crucify your King?</u> The chief priests answered, <u>We have no king but Caesar</u>.**

Jesus is the Anointed One and the Son of God. He will return as the eternal King of Israel, but He is led away to die.

Some people believe that God should have stopped the crucifixion of His Son. He certainly has the power to do so. However, they do not understand. Do you remember the example of the computer program? Once the program is executed, it runs until it is completed. In other words, it is God's will that His Son should die. What is God's reason for this? Later, when writing to those saved by the Gospel of the Kingdom, the Apostle Peter answers this question. 1 Peter 1:18-20:

> 18 **Forasmuch as ye know that <u>ye were not redeemed with corruptible things</u>, as silver and gold, from your vain conversation [living] received by [the] tradition from your fathers;**
>
> 19 **<u>But with the precious blood of Christ, as of a lamb without blemish and without spot</u>:**
>
> 20 **<u>Who verily was foreordained before the foundation of the world</u>, but was manifest [made known] in these last times for you,**

If this was a computer program, then God wrote before the earth was created.

Jesus is taken away to be crucified. John 19:16-18:

> 16 **Then delivered he him therefore unto them to be crucified. And they took Jesus, and led him away.**

17 And he bearing his cross went forth into a place called the place of a skull, which is called in the Hebrew Golgotha:

18 Where they crucified him, and two other with him, on either side one, and Jesus in the midst.

Many Jews argued that the sign placed on the Cross over Jesus' head was wrong. It was Pilate who sentenced Jesus to the crime for which He was charged by the Jews. Notice that they came to Pilate to complain about the sign. Verses 19-22:

19 And Pilate wrote a title, and put it on the cross. And the writing was, JESUS OF NAZARETH THE KING OF THE JEWS.

20 This title then read many of the Jews: for the place where Jesus was crucified was nigh to the city: and it was written in Hebrew, and Greek, and Latin.

21 Then said the chief priests of the Jews to Pilate, Write not, <u>The King of the Jews</u>; but that <u>he said, I am King of the Jews</u>.

22 **Pilate answered, <u>What I have written</u> <u>I have written.</u>**

His garments were divided among the soldiers. We would say that this was a high-profile case. The crowds came from far and wide because they knew Jesus and came to see what He would do. Verses 23-24:

> **23 Then the soldiers, when they had crucified Jesus, took his garments, and made four parts, to every soldier a part; and also his coat: now the coat was without seam, woven from the top throughout.**

> **24 They said therefore among themselves, Let us not rend it, but cast lots for it, whose it shall be: that the scripture might be fulfilled, which saith, They parted my raiment among them, and for my vesture they did cast lots. These things therefore the soldiers did.**

Many of those who followed Jesus and believed on Him stood in shock and grief. They wanted to stay with Him in His anguish and pain. Verses 25-27:

25 Now there stood by the cross of Jesus his mother, and his mother's sister, Mary the wife of Cleophas, and Mary Magdalene.

26 When Jesus therefore saw his mother, and the disciple standing by, whom he loved, he saith unto his mother, Woman, behold thy son!

27 Then saith he to the disciple, Behold thy mother! And from that hour that disciple took her unto his own home.

While Jesus remained alive on the Cross, we must remember that Jesus was also a Man. His simple words, "I thirst," show us His human frailty. Verses 28-30:

28 After this, Jesus knowing that all things were now accomplished, that the scripture might be fulfilled, saith, I thirst.

29 Now there was set a vessel full of vinegar: and they filled a spunge with vinegar, and put it upon hyssop, and put it to his mouth.

30 When Jesus therefore had received the vinegar, he said, <u>It is finished</u>: and he bowed his head, and gave up the ghost.

The Jews were concerned about the Passover which begins at sundown. So, they approached Pilate to expediate Jesus' death by breaking His legs. Jews know that the Passover Lamb must be perfect. The lamb must be without blemish, sin, and have no bones broken. Verses 31-35:

31 The Jews therefore, because it was the preparation, that the bodies should not remain upon the cross on the sabbath day, (for that sabbath day was an high day,) besought Pilate that their legs might be broken, and that they might be taken away.

32 Then came the soldiers, and brake the legs of the first, and of the other which was crucified with him. **33** But when they came to Jesus, and saw that he was dead already, they brake not his legs:

34 But one of the soldiers with a spear pierced his side, and forthwith came there out blood and water.

35 And he that saw it bare record, and his record is true: and he knoweth that he saith true, that ye might believe.

The person who "saw it and bare record" of the truth is the Apostle John, the author of the Gospel of John. He stood beside Mary, the mother of Jesus. Verses 36-37:

36 For these things were done, that the scripture should be fulfilled, A bone of him shall not be broken. **37** And again another scripture saith, They shall look on him whom they pierced.

What would be done with Jesus' body? God provided a man named Joseph of Arimathaea who owned an unused tomb. Verses 38-42:

38 And after this Joseph of Arimathaea, being a disciple of Jesus, but secretly for fear of the Jews, besought Pilate that he might take away the body of Jesus: and Pilate gave him leave [permission]. He came therefore, and took the body of Jesus.

39 And there came also Nicodemus, which at the first came to Jesus by night, and brought a mixture of myrrh and aloes, about an hundred pound weight.

40 Then took they the body of Jesus, and wound it in linen clothes with the spices, as the manner of the Jews is to bury.

41 Now in the place where he was crucified there was a garden; and in the garden a new sepulchre, wherein was never man yet laid.

42 There laid they Jesus therefore because of the Jews' preparation day; for the sepulchre was nigh at hand [near].

It is the Jewish custom to bury the dead before sundown on the day that they die. This was done hastily as it was near the start of Passover. They would return after the Sabbath to complete their preparation of the body. Needless to say, they did not know that the body would not be there.

22

John 20

In the previous chapter, Jesus' body was taken down for the Cross and quickly prepared for burial because of the Jewish burial customs. God is all-knowing. The women would return on the day following the Sabbath to prepare the body. John 20:1-10:

1 The first day of the week cometh Mary Magdalene early, when it was yet dark, unto the sepulchre, and seeth the stone taken away from the sepulchre.

2 Then she runneth, and cometh to Simon Peter, and to the other disciple, whom Jesus loved, and saith unto them, They have taken away the Lord out of the sepulchre, and we know not where they have laid him.

3 Peter therefore went forth, and that other disciple, and came to the sepulchre. 4 So they ran both together: and the other disciple did outrun Peter, and came first to the sepulchre.

5 And he stooping down, and looking in, saw the linen clothes lying; yet went he not in. 6 Then cometh Simon Peter following him, and went into the sepulchre, and seeth the linen clothes lie,

7 And the napkin, that was about his head, not lying with the linen clothes, but wrapped together in a place by itself. 8 Then went in also that other disciple, which came first to the sepulchre, and he saw, and believed.

9 For as yet they knew not the scripture, that he must rise again from the dead. 10 Then the disciples went away again unto their own home.

These believers viewed the interior of the tomb. It was not vandalized, but neatly organized. The burial clothes and napkin were laid out. They were in shock since they anticipated finding Jesus' corpse but instead they found the tomb empty. We find Mary outside crying. Verse 11:

> 11 **But Mary stood without at the sepulchre weeping: and as she wept, she stooped down, and looked into the sepulchre,**

She speaks with two men who are sitting inside the tomb. Verses 12-13:

> 12 **And seeth two angels in white sitting, the one at the head, and the other at the feet, where the body of Jesus had lain.**

> 13 **And they say unto her, Woman, why weepest thou? She saith unto them, Because they have taken away my Lord, and I know not where they have laid him.**

Mary is about to have the surprise of her life. Verse 14:

> 14 **And when she had thus said, she turned herself back, and saw Jesus standing, and knew not that it was Jesus.**

He speaks to her and she believes that He is the

gardener. A dialogue between them begins. Verses 15-17:

> 15 Jesus saith unto her, Woman, why weepest thou? whom seekest thou? She, supposing him to be the gardener, saith unto him, Sir, if thou have borne him hence, tell me where thou hast laid him, and I will take him away.

> 16 Jesus saith unto her, Mary. She turned herself, and saith unto him, Rabboni; which is to say, Master.

> 17 Jesus saith unto her, Touch me not; for I am not yet ascended to my Father: but go to my brethren, and say unto them, I ascend unto my Father, and your Father; and to my God, and your God.

She immediate went to report this to the disciples who were together grieving the loss of their Messiah. Verse 18:

> 18 Mary Magdalene came and told the disciples that she had seen the Lord, and that he had spoken these things unto her.

The Jewish Sabbath is on the seventh day because it honors the completion of God's Creation. No work can take place as this is the day of rest. Therefore, the women arrived at the tomb early on the first day of the week which we know as Sunday. It was Sunday evening when Jesus appears to His disciples in the flesh. Verse 19:

> 19 Then the same day at evening, being the first day of the week, when the doors were shut where the disciples were assembled for fear of the Jews, came Jesus and stood in the midst, and saith unto them, Peace be unto you.

Jesus shows them His wounds and they believe. Verses 20-23:

> 20 And when he had so said, he shewed unto them his hands and his side. Then were the disciples glad, when they saw the Lord.

> 21 Then said Jesus to them again, Peace be unto you: as my Father hath sent me, even [that is to say] so send I you.

> 22 And when he had said this, he breathed on them, and saith unto them,

Receive ye the Holy Ghost:

23 Whose soever sins ye remit [forgive], they are remitted [forgiven] unto them; and whose soever sins ye retain [keep], they are retained [kept].

One of the disciples was not there when Jesus appeared. He has been referred to as "doubting Thomas" because he wanted to see with his own eyes before he believed. Verses 24-25:

24 But Thomas, one of the twelve, called Didymus, was not with them when Jesus came.

25 The other disciples therefore said unto him, We have seen the Lord. But he said unto them, Except I shall see in his hands the print of the nails, and put my finger into the print of the nails, and thrust my hand into his side, I will not believe.

After a week, Jesus came again and He knew that Thomas had doubted. Verses 26-29:

26 And after eight days again his disciples were within, and Thomas with

them: then came Jesus, the doors being shut, and stood in the midst, and said, Peace be unto you.

27 Then saith he to Thomas, Reach hither thy finger, and behold my hands; and reach hither thy hand, and thrust it into my side: and be not faithless, but believing.

28 And Thomas answered and said unto him, <u>My Lord and my God</u>.

29 Jesus saith unto him, Thomas, because thou hast seen me, thou hast believed: blessed are they that have not seen, and yet have believed.

Miracles, signs, and wonders were done by Jesus as proof He was risen from the dead. Many of these are not recorded. Those that were written were recorded for one reason: that you might believe. Verses 30-31:

30 And many other signs truly did Jesus in the presence of his disciples, which are not written in this book:

31 But these are written, that ye might

believe that Jesus is the Christ, the Son of God; and that believing ye might have life through his name.

23

John 21

During Jesus' early ministry, He spend much of His time in the beautiful area surrounding the Sea of Galilee. It is here where He met the fishermen who would become "fishers of men." The Sea of Galilee has other names: Lake Kinneret, Lake of Gennesaret, and Lake Tiberias. It was here that Jesus told His disciples He would meet them. John 21:1-4:

1 **After these things Jesus shewed himself again to the disciples at the sea of Tiberias; and on this wise shewed he himself.**

2 **There were together Simon Peter, and Thomas called Didymus, and Nathanael of Cana in Galilee, and the sons of Zebedee, and two other of his disciples.**

3 Simon Peter saith unto them, I go a fishing. They say unto him, We also go with thee. They went forth, and entered into a ship immediately; and that night they caught nothing.

4 But when the morning was now come, Jesus stood on the shore: but the disciples knew not that it was Jesus.

The reference to two hundred cubits puts their distance from the shore at about three hundred feet. So, we can imagine this dialogue as some yelling going back and forth. Verses 5-6:

5 Then Jesus saith unto them, Children, have ye any meat? They answered him, No.

6 And he said unto them, Cast the net on the right side of the ship, and ye shall find. They cast therefore, and now they were not able to draw it for the multitude of fishes.

John, the author of this gospel, is first to recognize Jesus. Verse 7:

7 Therefore that disciple whom Jesus

loved saith unto Peter, It is the Lord. Now when Simon Peter heard that it was the Lord, he girt his fisher's coat unto him, (for he was naked,) and did cast himself into the sea.

With Peter jumping out of the boat, the others came to shore with their net filled with fish. Verses 8-14:

8 And the other disciples came in a little ship; (for they were not far from land, but as it were two hundred cubits,) dragging the net with fishes.

9 As soon then as they were come to land, they saw a fire of coals there, and fish laid thereon, and bread.

10 Jesus saith unto them, Bring of the fish which ye have now caught.

11 Simon Peter went up, and drew the net to land full of great fishes, an hundred and fifty and three: and for all there were so many, yet was not the net broken.

12 Jesus saith unto them, Come and dine. And none of the disciples durst

[dared to] ask him, Who art thou? knowing that it was the Lord.

13 Jesus then cometh, and taketh bread, and giveth them, and fish likewise.

14 This is now the third time that Jesus shewed himself to his disciples, after that he was risen from the dead.

As they sat around the cooking fire, they shared a meal like they had so many times before. Jesus asks Peter a question three times. He does this to engrain in Peter's mind the answers he gives to the Lord. Verses 15-17:

15 So when they had dined, Jesus saith to Simon Peter, Simon, son of Jonas, lovest thou me more than these? He saith unto him, Yea, Lord; thou knowest that I love thee. He saith unto him, Feed my lambs.

16 He saith to him again the second time, Simon, son of Jonas, lovest thou me? He saith unto him, Yea, Lord; thou knowest that I love thee. He saith unto him, Feed my sheep.

17 He saith unto him the third time, Simon, son of Jonas, lovest thou me? Peter was grieved because he said unto him the third time, Lovest thou me? And he said unto him, Lord, thou knowest all things; thou knowest that I love thee. Jesus saith unto him, <u>Feed my sheep</u>.

We are going to pause for a moment because what Jesus is saying to Peter has to do with his future. When Jesus uses the words "lambs" and "sheep" to whom is He referring? It has to do with Jesus mission and that mission is being transferred to the disciples of whom Peter is one. Remember, Jesus is the Shepherd of Israel. Consider two scriptural references:

Matthew 10:5-7:

> **5** These twelve Jesus sent forth, and commanded them, saying, Go not into the way of the Gentiles, and into any city of the Samaritans enter ye not: **6** <u>But go rather to the lost sheep of the house of Israel</u>. **7** And as ye go, <u>preach, saying, The kingdom of heaven is at hand</u>.

Matthew 15:24:

24 **But he answered and said, I am not sent but [except] unto the lost sheep of the house of Israel.**

Jesus' mission was determined before Creation. I would recommend you read the story of Isaiah's Suffering Servant. (See Isaiah 53.) Jesus' purpose was proclaimed to the Jews by this prophet nearly seven hundred years before the birth of Jesus. This prophecy was spoken to Israel. Isaiah 53:6:

6 <u>**All we like sheep have gone astray; we**</u> **have turned every one to his own way;** <u>**and the LORD hath laid on him the in-**</u><u>**iquity of us all.**</u>

We return to our text. Jesus tells His disciples what to expect in their future as they serve Him. John 21:18-20:

18 **Verily, verily, I say unto thee, When thou wast young, thou girdedst thyself, and walkedst whither thou wouldest: but when thou shalt be old, thou shalt stretch forth thy hands, and another shall gird thee, and carry thee whither thou wouldest not.**

19 **This spake he, signifying by what**

death he should glorify God. And when he had spoken this, he saith unto him, Follow me.

20 Then Peter, turning about, seeth the disciple [John] whom Jesus loved following; which also leaned on his breast at supper, and said, Lord, which is he that betrayeth thee?

Peter looked at the Apostle John and basically asks Jesus, "What about him?" Verses 21-22:

21 Peter seeing him saith to Jesus, Lord, and what shall this man do?

22 Jesus saith unto him, If I will that he tarry till I come, what is that to thee? follow thou me.

Jesus' response that it is none of his concern is misinterpreted. Verse 23:

23 Then went this saying abroad among the brethren, that that disciple should not die: yet Jesus said not unto him, He shall not die; but, If I will that he tarry till I come, what is that to thee?

This disciple was the Apostle John who is the author of this gospel. It is he who recorded his testimony for our benefit. Verses 24-25:

24 This is the disciple which testifieth of these things, and wrote these things: and we know that his testimony is true.

25 And there are also many other things which Jesus did, the which, if they should be written every one, I suppose that even the world itself could not contain the books that should be written. Amen.

Epilogue

The Apostle John recorded his eyewitness account in his gospel which is different from the other gospels. The three previous gospels recorded by Matthew, Mark, and Luke are called the synoptic gospels for a reason. These other writers followed a similar format that recounts the life, teaching, and work of Jesus Christ's earthly ministry. As such, the placement of John's gospel in Scripture builds upon the historical narratives written by the others. John's gospel focuses on having faith in Jesus Christ—the Messiah and the Son of God.

There is material in the other gospels that John chose not to include. It is not that this material was unimportant, but it was already covered in the others. These omissions include His testing in the wilderness, Jesus' transfiguration, the discourse during the Lord's Supper, the Sermon on the Mount, and exorcisms of demons. Also, the Lord's Prayer and many of Jesus' parables are not found in his gospel. From the beginning of John's gospel, we find that his purpose is to present one simple truth: Jesus Christ is God Himself!

John makes the deity of Jesus clear from the opening verses of his gospel. John 1:1-5:

> 1 **In the beginning was the Word, and the Word was with God, and the Word was God.**
>
> 2 **The same was in the beginning with God.**
>
> 3 **All things were made by him; and without him was not any thing made that was made.**
>
> 4 **In him was life; and the life was the light of men.**
>
> 5 **And the light shineth in darkness; and the darkness comprehended it not.**

Throughout his gospel, John continually connects Jesus to the name of God. God told Moses His name. Exodus 3:14:

> 14 **And God said unto Moses, I AM THAT I AM: and he said, Thus shalt**

thou say unto the children of Israel, I AM hath sent me unto you.

John uses the name "I AM" throughout his gospel to establish the deity of Jesus. Below are some examples:

"I am the bread of life" (v. 6:35)
"I am the living bread" (v. 6:51)
"I am the light of the world" (v. 8:12)
"I am one that bears witness . . ." (v. 8:18)
"I am from above" (v. 8:23)
"Before Abraham was, I am" (v.8:58)
"I am the light of the world" (v. 9:5)
"I am the door of the sheep" (v. 10:7)
"I am the door" (v. 10:9)
"I am come that they might have life (v. 10:10)
"I am the good shepherd" (vs. 10:11,14)
"I am the Son of God" (v. 10:36)
"I am the resurrection, and the life" (v. 11:25)
"I am the way, the truth, and the life" (v. 14:6)
"I am in the Father" (v. 14:11)
"I am the true vine" (v. 15:1)

There is another reference to "I AM" which is perhaps the most poignant. It is only found in John's gospel. John 18:3-6:

3 Judas then, having received a band of men and officers from the chief priests and Pharisees, cometh thither with lanterns and torches and weapons.

4 Jesus therefore, knowing all things that should come upon him, went forth, and said unto them, Whom seek ye?

5 They answered him, Jesus of Nazareth. Jesus saith unto them, <u>I am</u> he. And Judas also, which betrayed him, stood with them.

6 As soon then as he had said unto them, <u>I am</u> he, they went backward, and fell to the ground.

There it is. Jesus used the name of God to answer them and they all fell backwards.

The Gospel of John stands apart from the other three gospels for good reason. The others provide eyewitness testimony that Jesus is the Messiah of Israel and the Son of God. However. John sought to prove that the same "I AM" Who sent Moses to deliver Israel from Egypt is the same "I AM" Who came to save Israel from their sins.

Other GraceWord Publications

In English:

1st Corinthians: Dispensationally Considered
1st & 2nd Thessalonians: Dispensationally Con.
1st & 2nd Timothy & Titus: Dispensationally Con.
2nd Corinthians: Dispensationally Considered
Acts: Dispensationally Considered
Colossians & Philemon: Dispensationally Con.
Ephesians: Dispensationally Considered
Galatians: Dispensationally Considered
Hebrews: Dispensationally Considered
How Am I Wired?
Letters To Theophilus
Philippians: Dispensationally Considered
Romans: Dispensationally Considered
The Glorious Destiny Of Israel
The Gospel of Luke: Dispensationally Con.
The Gospel of Mark: Dispensationally Con.
The Gospel of Matthew: Dispensationally Con.
The Hidden Gospel
The Seven Hebrew Epistles: Dispensationally Con.

Two Distinct Gospel Messages Of The New Test.

En español:

Cartas A Teófilo
Efesios: Dispensacionalmente considerado
El evangelio Oculto: Una vez fue un misterio . . .

About The Author

Dr. David Alan Greene has over thirty-five years of experience as an insurance agent selling both property and casualty as well as life insurance. During his career, he taught and explained the content and meaning of policies to his clients. Now retired, he devotes much of his time to teaching the Bible.

He obtained his Bachelor of Theology, Master of Biblical Studies, and Ph.D. in Biblical Studies from Evangelical Theological Seminary where he holds the position of Dean of Graduate Studies. He also holds a Ph.D. in Christian Counseling. He has written numerous biblical commentaries and books on rightly dividing the Word of Truth.